The Light in a New Age

Meditations on the Oneness of the Church of Love and Extracts from a *Diary of Discovery and Revelations* compiled by the writer from mid-June 1973: the 600th anniversary of St Julian of Norwich, England: Divine Revelations.

"For you who read and I who write and Love are One!"

(From a quotation for which we are most grateful to whom I know not.)

Jesus Christ, of the Godhead III, Lord of all, you sent us your winged messengers of Heaven from the west, in mid-June 1973, when three concentric circles of seagulls flying in perfect wing beat uniSon, appeared high over our stable calling to us. On looking up they banked to fly in uniSon of three, home to the west, the chalk hill cliffs of our Sussex coast.

(It was the 600th anniversary of Mother Julian [St Julian] of Norwich's Divine experiences of the 'Passion of Our Lord', of sixteen visions and revelations of the Godhead of Love.) The gulls were gyrating in a clockwise direction looking forward in time.

Jesus of our Godhead III, the following year, in mid-February 1974, from the west, on a stormy day. You sent us a very large circle of shrieking gulls, low overhead. Now flying erratically and in a clockwise (yet up and down, east to west, and north to south) direction, as before, they again banked returning to the west, the white coastal cliffs of our Sussex coast, linking Brighton to Eastbourne, Sussex. Jesus, these flights were prophetic for as I meditated on your three circles of 15th June 1973, the Message of Love to my soul was, "I am the One Church, in the One World, in the One Universe." Yet the message of these from our God of Love, the shrieking gulls, revealed the cries of dying Christians in Ireland, and in other countries of the world.

One Godhead of Three in the Unity of Love,
Power and Glory.

(For Jesus said, "Him that cometh unto me I will in no way cast out.")

(For from my birth in Devonshire up until now I have been discovering His oneness of our glorious Godhead of God, in all Creation and the Word Revealed. The Unity of our Lord of Love and God are One.)

Forthwith and shown by the Bible as the prime source of Grace and Worship and Healing of Divisions: Unity, throughout the Nations upon the Earth. For throughout every year of my life I have been discovering the wonder and the Glory of God in all Creation, and the Word Revealed: for it has always been in simplicity there lies that greater 'Glory', the 'Oneness of Love, Unity and Eternity'!

Jesus' Love for all mankind, the Godhead III. For on the 15th day of June, 1973, God sent three concentric circles of seagulls over our stable, they banked and flew home westwards. Again on this Holy Cross Acre God has granted six messages to my soul. For on a mid-February day in 1974 I stood on the site of the three mystical ley line intersections. Then God sent a huge circle of seagulls screaming loudly, but gyrating in a clockwise direction (looking forward in time). They were most erratic in flight, up and down, to and fro. As I looked Heavenwards they banked to fly home to the Sussex coast, and the West, when our God of Love spoke to my soul, "I am the One church, in the One world, in the One Universe." Again, Amazing Grace.

A foreknowledge of the One church of Love of the third millennium, Unity.

Thus after almost twenty-one years of Divine Revelations concerning Unity to come, God once again confirms His message of Love to all mankind. Foretold and experienced here on the three cross site († T +) on the 15th June, 1975. "I am the One church, in the One world, in the One Universe." For then God sent three concentric circles of seagulls from the west over our small stable when they banked and flew back home. (For the mark on my left wrist changes from time to time, then a 3 (three) then the (T) symbolises resurrection, and the dark spot (•) where Jesus was nailed to the cross.

June to early July 1975, in the dream I landed in the centre of a very large set-up of Christian people gathered together in the open, praying to God for Unity, seemingly in the centre of Ireland.

I was then caught up in a true Love feast of an open air Holy Lord's Supper, Communion, or Mass service where those participating gathered thin wafers of home-baked bread from a large velvet cushion. Standing in the centre of this gathering as the cushion was being passed around by four men, I noticed that on receipt of the Host (bread) the communicants burst into Songs and hymns of Joy and were highly ecstatic, leaping and throwing up their arms following the message of Love which I had first given them: that I had experienced a visitation of the loving head of Christ of the Holy Shroud, and the Father in a trance, and had witnessed a circle of light on our lawn indicating the oneness and wholeness of God's One Church of Love. Also I spoke of the glorious revelation of our risen Lord within the Godhead early on Easter morning with ten Disciples in the Supper chamber.

(That together with his two Disciples and three Mary's? I too had seen our Lord God of the One Holy Church of Love).

Also I spoke of the granting of a Latin cross of hazel twigs on our lawn on 15th June, 1975, pointing to the east. Filled with the spirit and pain of the soul, the Lord led me to record these experiences of the Light, Truth and Life and of those to come (after the soul message, "Write a diary of Discovery and Revelations").

(For three days and nights the soul pain was constant when I wrote sixty-five A4 pages of experiences from my birth in Devon until mid-June 1975.) For each morning I crossed the lawn towards the site of the three crosses and each time Dear Lord you embraced my right arm and led me back into our home to continue writing.

The message then I feel was one of true spiritual Love transcending all Christian doctrine, uniting us with Him in His One kingdom of Love. A prophetic revelation that Anglicans, Catholics, and all branches of the 'One True Vine' will One day unite, for this is God's will for us all. Also that other Faiths and Churches of the east will join with those of the west spanning the whole circle of the earth of the Godhead III to come, also the north and the south.

The north with the south... Yahweh (God) said, "Turning to the Jews who had believed in Him, Jesus said, "If you dwell within the revelation I have brought, you are indeed my Disciples: you shall know the Truth, and the Truth will set you free." John VIII v.31.

"Listen now to my words, if any man among you is a prophet I make myself known to him in a vision, I speak to him in a vision, I speak to him in a dream. Not so with my servant Moses: he is at home in my house, I speak to him face to face, plainly and not in riddles, and he sees the form of Yahweh." Numbers 12, 6-8.

"Till we all come to the Unity of the faith and the knowledge of the Son of God, to a perfect man, to the measure of the stature of the fullness of Christ." Ephesians IV v13

Approaching Christmas, 1974

Once again childhood experiences transcend the space of time, with the valleys echoing the Christmas bells, both near and far, as the pure light shines out of the mist enshrouding the timeless hills. Born anew of the One church of Love, the message of the Christ-child goes forth to the whole world, "I am One church of Love, One world of Love, One Universal Love."

One Godhead over all.

(The new man [Ephesians 4.13] "Till we all come to the Unity of the faith and the knowledge of the Son of God, to a perfect man, to the measure of the stature of the fullness of Christ.")

"Thanks be to God, forever," I cry.

An Extract from our Diary of Discovery and Revelation from mid-June 1973 of the Convictions and Spiritual Insights of a Member of the Church of Love

After a period of three days (mid-June 1975) of spiritual direction (soul pain) following the mystical presentation of a Latin cross of twigs by my feet on our lawn pointing to the east, some sixty-five foolscap pages were written from which the following is an extract. For this was the message to my soul as I stooped down, "Write a Diary of Discovery and Revelation," and caught by the right arm I was twisted round and led back into our house.

"From my early childhood days on a farm in Devon and here in the southernmost county of Sussex, England, at the age of five I now recall some of the beautiful and arresting discoveries of the effects of the sun and light shining forth upon a meadow, early one summer morning in June, in my early youth on a farm at Ripe. A scene of gossamer plants was covered by many miles of spider webs woven all night through.

What pearls of worth snatched from the depths of the ocean could be compared with the many thousand, thousands of sparkling dew drops of rainbow right over a field of flowering grasses and some weeds, one early morning on an early June summer's day. The whole field was swaying gracefully with the purest of gentle breezes and sparkling with millions of dew drop pearls, it appeared, touched by the new born rays of the sun, creeping over the nearby high hedgerow on the eastern side of the field. Each drop of dew being more beautiful and more exotic than any delicate pearl couched in the womb of its mother's shell. These suspended liquid pearl-like dew drops in their millions it appeared, could be seen hanging from every minute thread of the woven webs, linked by an endless chain of taut silken anchors and ties from the many tall flowering grasses and a few weeds. This whole field of many acres was thus covered with this gossamer veil of enmeshed webs cast by a vast army of industrious spiders probably working at fantastic speeds throughout the night? To what purpose one might ask? Yet one could only stand and stare, caught up in the wonder and glorious beauty of it all. Could it have been a reflection of the 'Eternal city'? "Yes!" I cry! For all is Revelation if we truly Love Him who Loves us all as One. The oneness of Christ and the Father of Love the Godhead III. Today I feel that there was hidden messages for the church in that vast veil of spiders webs covering the face of the earth. Each pearl symbolising a pearl of a departed soul living in Glory I thought?

As the sun's bright searching rays crept over the high hedgerows, each drop of liquid pearl splashed countless diamond studded rays of reflected light, glowing with every colour of the spectrum from the webs, in all directions, all over the mass of grasses, weeds and herbs. And so this scene of panoramic beauty of scintillating rainbow lights increased in colour and intensity, and sparkled like the wave-tops of some vast ocean controlled by the Creator of Light. Such is the wonder, beauty, and Glory of Creation. The light and warmth of the sun, with the rain and the wind, are so inextricably interwoven that only the nature of God's creation can truly acknowledge these Heavenly gifts.

To return to the two-hour trance of 18 February 1976, I feel the reader may wish to read this. On the left hand our Dear Lord marked my left wrist underneath with an 'R' (resurrection) and close by a dark circular form central indicating where Jesus' wrist was nailed to the cross and not the hands which many artists have painted or carved throughout history of Jesus on the cross. Three days later it was clearly visible. On the back of my right hand the skin was scratched, leaving an open sore which discharged a little water and blood most days. This was miraculously healed, twelve months later, at night, for I was amazed to see my hand healed the next day.

Four recorded Divine Godhead Revelations have been granted to my soul Easter 1976 to Easter 1977. I have painted the Lord's Last Supper, most prophetic, but not the Godhead over all. I have been led to paint one only to date, painted in Hannover, Germany. Jesus appeared in the chamber after His Resurrection to ten awaiting Disciples.

A year later in July 1978 a small patch of hard skin appeared on the back of my right hand. This grew into the form of a trefoil ivy-leaf I sensed. It came off just before Beth and I joined an Ecumenical Pilgrimage to Southern Ireland, Easter 1986; eight Catholics and three Anglicans I believe. We visited a light centre in southern Ireland, but it was at Knock, staying in a youth hostel, one night, after reading a portion from the Bible, God filled me with the Holy Spirit, foretelling Healing to come to Ireland by the end of 2000 years of Christ? (A united Ireland, I trust).

Three Centres of Light (August 1976 - 2nd Feb 1982)

Lourdes, France: Fatima, Portugal: Knock, Ireland (19th and early 20th centuries)

1. Of Lourdes, France (1858)

Bernadette Soubirous when a young girl, experienced her first vision of a lady, Mary, on the 11th February 1858. The visions continued until March, the third month of that year (my birthday month).

At 9 p.m. on the evening of the 24th or 25th August 1976 I had read my Bible and was reading 'The voice of Lourdes' and on reaching page 13, "The water saw thee O God. The waters trembled at the sight of thee moved to their inmost depth," (Psalm 76: 17) and on continuing to read, I was instantly filled with the spirit on reading the words, "quite suddenly she heard the sound of a rushing wind," and my body stiffened as I read. On reaching the end of the verse, the spirit of Love left my body. (God thus confirmed Bernadette's experience of the soul at Lourdes, France.)

This was an experience of Revelation of the Truth of Lourdes, the light healing centre at the foot of the Pyrenees, France. The third vision was granted to Bernadette there on the third reciting of the Rosary in the third month of that year of 1858. (The symbol of three has become more and more meaningful from my birth, in each year of my life, and thirteen, the mystical number in my life from birth also, I believe.)

Bernadette's experiences were those granted by our Godhead of the One church of Love. Similar visions have equally been granted to us living here in God's garden home. Earlier still in 1373, of those of Mother Julian of Norwich who was granted sixteen visions of Divine Love of the passion of Christ. St Julian the forerunner of the Divine revelations granted to us and on and above this Holy acre since 15th June 1973, the 600th anniversary of St Julian of Norwich, England. For all Revelations granted here are a continuation of hers.

Last night I was awakened to experience with the soul a large dense black head form from the window in the north wall of our bedroom, where Jesus' head appeared, in the napkin for two hours, eyes ablaze, midnight, 18 July 1976.

Now, believing it to be the anti-Christ, I cried out from the soul, "Get you behind me Satan," and crossed myself: "In the name of the Father and of the Son and of the Holy Spirit." Instantly a crucifix (about nine inches high) appeared in the head, central and both Christ's body and the cross, and twelve edges revealed tongues of golden light throughout. The vision glowed and faded and reappeared twice more in like manner. Full of golden light, each time it was of the symbol of three. The crucifix of the Eternal Love to all nations.

Six days later, the Very Reverend Bishop Tutu was enthroned Bishop of Johannesburg, South Africa. Thus God granted I feel foreknowledge of a golden age to come of freedom and Peace for all nations, and Peace and Unity in Africa to come. ("Declare... His wonders among all people." Psalm 96,3)

John VI v 5, 6, 7
Feeding the 5,000, 18th June 1976

I have since been led to meditate on Jesus' call to my soul in the two hour trance on July 18th 1976 (three messages).

No 3: Feeding the Nations – the Third Message

"Communicate the Experience to all nations."

These three Divine calls occurred on the 603rd anniversary of those of St Julian of Norwich, England in 1373. For then in 1973 God sent to us here three concentric circles of seagulls on 15th June 1973, flying in perfect wing beat formation from the west and banking over our stable they then flew back to the west, the white cliffs of the Sussex coast no doubt?

So I strongly suggest that readers of our experiences (of Beth and myself) should first read and meditate on those Revelations recorded by St Julian in 1373. Hers occurred over a period of eighteen years I believe, and so may ours, for, perhaps for some twenty-one years?

And so I believe that all, so far granted to us, may continue. From my birth at 'Weycroft', Devon on 31 March 1916, I have always been seeking reality for I believe in Predestination – called by God, before birth. Also, at the age of four, God spoke to my soul at Kinders Farm, Devon. "Stand up for Truth and Justice."

Round about the 1960s I grew to Love a popular Song from the radio:
"Why do you whisper green grass, why tell the trees all ain't so?" (It always transported me back to my childhood days, for it was registered in my soul, no doubt?)

One Holy Church of Love

One Word, One Life, One Spirit,
One Church of Love is Unity to Come,

(His Amazing Grace, Midnight July 18th 1976
Jesus' head wrapped in the napkin of the tomb)

Jesus, Lord, I am that sin which nailed You to the cross.
In Love you came to us at night wrapped in the Holy Shroud of Death, Rebirth and Life, your head bound, with the napkin of the tomb, and your eyes of light Divine. Jesus your Light and Love surrounds us now, from that night in June, when you appeared in our home from Calvary's tomb, you filled our souls with Love. Glorified by the Father, born again from that tomb:

You came to us on reading your word of Light. Maccabees 1, chapter 13, Purification of the temple. Jesus we Love you as One. (The Jerusalem Bible).

Jesus Christ, the blazing radiance of your Eyes of Light and Love filled my soul, transfixed with fear and awe, for two hours and more as you moved close to my eyes and then to and from the north window, north to south and south to north. Finally you left us to pass over us, through to the east to west and north to south. Jesus, your Love pierced the darkness of this world of sin, revealing Eternal life of Love, Truth and life, reborn from the tomb.
Lord, we Love you as One.
Jesus, you held me spellbound in this trance of blinding light of open radiant eyes, followed by cosmic sun-like rays of living Light and Truth (the radiant Son of God) in a spiritual sun of blazing light, appearing where your head was seen.
Jesus, you and the Father of Love came as 'One in Glory' for you closed my human eyes before your radiant sun, pinching my eyelids so tight!
As with Moses on the mountain top and Paul on the Damascus Road, Eternal light. Finally, shedding a Heavenly circle of golden light upon your garden-home.
Revealing God is One, of both Testaments, Old and New.

Jesus, I was so unworthy of the touch of your presence for I cried out, "Lord, here I am; what shall I do?"

Jesus, we Love you as One dear Lord and Father of all life, the Word, and Sacrament of Love and of Wisdom overall. Jesus, with your Love we were Christed, made one with you Lord of all. Lord, we Love you as One, for you called me at the age of four: "Come follow me" (in effect 'standing up for Truth and Justice' at Kinders farm Devon, as called – autumn 1920).

Jesus, your loving presence filled my soul with pain, causing me to clasp the Bible to my chest in fear and awe: to cry out from the soul, "My hair is white in an aura of light," one Christ-church of Love. Jesus, your loving arms lifted up my weary hands over the word of life (Bible), touching my hands as one in yours, and yours in mine of light and Love Eternal. (The next day at the end of the nerve extremity was an open wound where on the back of the right hand water and blood came forth from that night onwards for one whole year.) It was healed by God exactly twelve months later.

Jesus, your loving touch left this stigmata on the back of my right hand and an imprint of a nail wound on the left wrist, confirming your death on the cross.

Christ, we Love you as One, One Christ-head, One spiritual Son of blazing light, One circle of light from our God, of the Godhead, three in One, One Love, One Church in the Unity of three.

Jesus Divine, the Love, Joy, Hope and Peace of your Eternal transcending light can never fade or die. Jesus with each daily sunset we see you rise again in Glory, this for all the world to see, for you and the Father as One. Jesus, with your Love you gave us freedom and Peace which the world cannot give.

Father Divine, your church of Love, is One in Unity. For One all glorious Godhead reigns supreme.

(Paul said, "When it (the Heart) is turned to the Lord the veil (over God's face) shall be taken away." 2 Corinthians, 3:16).

Jesus in Love Divine, you changed my human and spiritual life from this trance as with Paul on the Damascus road. A call to change direction – for all mankind.

(1) You separated me spiritually from all man's institutions (and I shared in all forms of worship, anchored to the One Book of Love, the Holy Bible.

(2) Being advanced of the soul by God to the end of the century (2000 years of Christ). A prophetic message for all, life Eternal, The Godhead III.

(3) You also directed me to communicate these all-glorious experiences of the soul to All Nations. The One church is Unity, of the Godhead III, of Love.

Thus you revealed your will for all mankind. To work and pray for the spiritual oneness of the One all-glorious Godhead III the first early church in Unity. For Love is the Power and the Glory of God and Christ in Unity. Your call before Abraham was, "I am," I have Eternal Love Divine – Love is Unity – One Church Eternal."

Mary who Loves us all as One with Christ her Son
Friday 3 June, 1977

Following a reading of the Word I laid down the Bible to pray Our Lord's prayer of Love, filled with His loving presence and fully awake. There suddenly appeared in the east window of visions from Heaven, a head of a woman with dark curly hair, fading and then reappearing more as of human form, it was revealed again and it continued for a time, how long I could not say, of the soul, and of timelessness.

Suddenly the scene changed for this loving woman was Mary, our Lord's Mother? Dressed now in a dark hood, bending over a crib or cradle on the floor. The crib was covered with a hood with one end open, facing the east; and inside was lying our dear Lord facing the east? I do not really know for Mary was not clearly revealed, now as with our dear Lord's head of the Holy Shroud in July 1976.

This vision was again suddenly more sharply defined, then it faded, as of a grey light of the soul. Then the form was once again more clearly revealed. Then it faded once more for this scene was of the 'Unity of Three'. A revelation of the perfect Mother with the Christ child, Jesus our Saviour, or was it of Elizabeth and John the Baptist? But no, the face and features of Elizabeth would have appeared as an older woman: Mary revealed three times over, confirmed by God, of youth and Love.

Read John 8 v31.

("My soul has magnified the Lord for my spirit has rejoiced in God my Saviour," dear Mary's prayer).

("There shall come forth a rod out of the stem of Jesse and a branch shall grow out of his roots," Isaiah XI-1).

July 1977

On the morning following the first anniversary of the midnight trance, July 18th 1976, I was amazed to see that the open wound on the back of my right hand had healed perfectly during the night! God's healing Power through patience and Love, for no ointment, if applied, could heal this open wound. From this time onward on the back of the right hand, about one inch to the right of the second nerve extremity, a small, at first minute, spot of skin began to grow. It continued so for many months to come until February-March 1983, when it revealed a dense growth of skin the form of which was that of an Ivy, or a trefoil leaf. (Eternity.)

Easter 1983

A week or two before I set out with Beth and nine of the pilgrims on an Evangelical pilgrimage to Knock, southern Ireland, this ivy leaf form of growth came off, when I was having a bath. Thus it appeared to develop over a period of six years and eight months from the experience of the trance?

Only God knows for it may have taken seven years to grow? The symbol from the Old Testament?

Jesus' promise to all mankind read John 14, v 21

"He that hath my commandments and keeps them, he it is that loveth me and he that loves me shall be loved by my Father, and I shall Love him and show myself to him."

**The Godhead of Love is One
(soul-travel) 6th August 1977**

Jesus, in your amazing Love you first revealed yourself with your Disciples at supper, on the night of the 6 August 1977, through your light to my soul. Thanks be to God.

Jesus, last night in a 'halo of light' you awakened me when you appeared in a white robe, standing with your chosen Disciples dressed in soft grey robes, they were seated on your left and right on both sides of the table, a deep white supper table, on one occasion, before your sacrifice Lord. After a time, this apparition faded and reappeared once again. I fell 'asleep' in your Peace Lord.

Father of all we Love you in Unity.

Jesus, early on Easter morn at 5 a.m. the following year (1978) you again filled our home with radiant light from the supper chamber, of soul-travel, when you burst through the east wall risen and glorified from the tomb. You first led me past your Disciples in grey, with five standing on either side of the white table, then, facing the east wall, I was elevated (with arms outstretched) to the ceiling. You then burst through the dissolving wall it seemed, full of radiant Glory, robed in gleaming rays of Eternal light, risen from the tomb. You also appeared with outstretched arms and hands as of the Unity of the Latin and Tau cross, I sensed of the Godhead form.

Father of all we Love you as One church of Love.

Jesus on this all-glorious morn you appeared as one Eternal Light crowned with a circlet of black spiky thorns of Friday's crucifixion, the mystic crown from God for you had risen from the Shroud and tomb. Jesus you filled my heart and soul with Joy; for your Love transcendent is ever with us now, for you alone have kept your promise Lord. The One church, in the One world, in the One Universe, Eternal Glory.

"If I be lifted up I will draw all men unto Me."

God revealing the oneness of the soul, anchored to Christ of the Godhead III, 'Resurrection', for this whole scene was framed within a side view of a massive human head, as of a lining of a telescope? Looking back through 2000 years (almost) of Christian worship, praise and adoration. One church of the all-glorious Godhead three to come, confirmed by God's message to my soul mid-February 1974.

Revealing the Godhead of Love is One in Unity, from that time onward.

"The same day at evening, being the first day of the week, when the doors were shut where the Disciples were assembled for fear of the Jews, came Jesus and stood in their midst, and said unto them, 'Peace be unto you.' And when he had so said, he showed unto them his hands and his side. Then were the Disciples glad, when they saw the Lord." (John XX – 19-20)

(We thank you our Godhead of Love)

Jesus, in all your Glory three nights later, you again appeared in a second experience of soul-travel, on my birthday, March 31st (1978), standing with your arms outstretched across the supper table of white.

Jesus, I believe you were showing two darkly-robed Disciples your wounded wrists and hands, for in the spirit I stood behind these two, for I was not to see your face of Love and Glory again? The whole scene was again magnified, within the outline of a human head, also you filled the chamber with your Eternal light.

One Godhead, Eternal, overall, the Unity of One Church of Love.

September 1978

Standing on the three cross site to come, by day, as the swallows were diving and weaving circles overhead, God spoke to my soul, "One day will be born a United States of Africa."

Jesus, Eternal light, with your chosen ones, you again appeared at 10.20 p.m. (September 13th 1978, the anniversary of the martyr St Cyprian of Carthage, Bishop, AD258). When we were fully awake, on this eve of Holy Cross Day, after reading from the word of life, Beth said, "Tomorrow is Holy Cross Day, shall we go to Communion?" Thus once again I have the conviction that this Holy Cross Church, Uckfield, is linked with the Holy Cross Acre, here).

Jesus full of light you were now seated with your Disciples and one was standing, Peter I sensed, the cup-bearer, in a lighter garment standing on your right. Once again the mystical scene of the Godhead in the Supper room of Light. Jesus dear Lord you confirmed this scene in a visit to the crypt of St Peter's, Rome, (when we prayed the Lord's Prayer) at Peter's tomb, (May 1980). (Focolare gathering, RC)

Jesus in Unity your church of Love is One.

Jesus, on the night of the 14th March 1979, you appeared at supper with your Disciples, in the Supper room in the all-glorious Godhead for the fourth time, revealing Jesus, that you and the Father are One in the Holy Eucharist, and the Mass and Lord's supper in the Unity of the loving Godhead. Thus the Lord's Supper is the most meaningful of all, to us!

One sacrament of Love in Unity, of word and Truth, of the Inspired, Prophetic and Revealed word of Love. (The soul truly reveals reality, His will, Jesus' Truth, Amazing Grace of God.

Father of all we Love you as One in Unity.

("He that believes in the Son has life and shall not come into judgement, for he whom his heart receives me, receives him who has sent me, for whom the Son makes free, shall be free indeed, because he has passed from death into life and he will receive from the Father, the spirit of Truth, which will lead us into all Truth, my Truth.")

21st July 1979
4 p.m.

At 3 p.m. today I fell into a deep sleep after meditating on bird flight phenomena, especially of three Brent geese passing low overhead, over the cosmic cross site here on 22nd April this year. (This day I had been feeling unwell, so weak in fact, the soul in trouble?)

Between 3-4 p.m. I experienced a strange dream of being taken up as a bird on an aerial flight westwards to the Lovely (though always not Peaceful) scenic island of Ireland. As it were a return visit, for we had spent a very happy camping holiday of exploration in Southern Ireland last year: some three weeks from Easter 1979.

(Easter 3rd May 1981) John 8, v 31

Fellowship Meeting with the Focalare in Rome

The day before we visited the Crypt of St Peter, Rome, we attended a great gathering of some 27,000 persons from sixty nations of the world, where Chiara, founder of the Focolare Evangelical Movement RC was addressing those present. The theme was 'The family and Love'. Towards the end of the day the Pope John II was greeted by Chiara and after a time he suddenly turned away from speaking to her and threw out his arms/hands towards the assembly saying, I believe, "I wish you were the church". Immediately I was filled with the Holy Spirit of Love of the Godhead III. Thus God confirmed my faith rooted in the oneness of Creation, and the Holy Bible, Christ and the revealed word of God. For all numbers divisible by three, from my birth have been of greater significance than others. For at the age of four I stayed for a few weeks at my grandparents' farm 'Kinders', Devon where God spoke to my soul, "Stand up for Truth and Justice," the Divine call to Love our neighbours and the Holy Bible of Love.

One Well of Living Water, One Life Eternal

22 March 1980

Following a silent Communion (in a town to the east of Sussex) last evening, I read chapter 13 of Revelations. I prayed and then laid the Bible down to go to sleep. The bright moon lighting the Heavens also filled our room with light, when suddenly, instantly, all was dark, when the spirit of Eternal light extinguished the Heavenly lamp and a brilliant warm spiritual light filled the centre of our east window as I lay in our bed.

This window of soul revelations from Heaven now revealed a woman, sitting on a stool or stone, close by rocks and a well. The soul indicated as she stood up, it was the Woman of Samaria, holding a large pitcher, poised in her arms when suddenly the liquid water and the large water pot glowed with a golden light as she poured water into a small flat dish held by the two hands of a figure standing in the deep (our Lord) shadow of a tree. Thus God revealed that in the realm of silence His golden light of Revelation may be granted to all, for God's word is one of Love.

Just as the water pot glowed with a golden light I knew the stranger to be our Lord begging for water from the Woman of Samaria at Jacob's well in Sychar. Jesus surprised this Samaritan woman whose people were despised by the Jews, and He spoke to her.

"If you only knew what a wonderful gift God has for you and who I am, you would ask for some living water." (John IV 1-46).

Thus God revealed his will to us, that we, (Beth and I) were to challenge the institutional churches, according to the visions granted, to seek Universal Renewal through the Godhead of all Love and Unity, to share in one United Reformed Church of the Loving Christ and God in Unity. Only the spirit of Truth can make us free for such is the will of God, to Love God and our neighbour as One and "I am the vine ye are the branches", as foretold by Jesus.

Yes, for all branches of the 'One True Vine' are to return to the Holy Bible form of worship.

From Daniel 12, 1-4, we can learn that just before the establishment of God's Universal Kingdom the world will experience a time of great trouble "such as never was" and would come at a time when knowledge would be increased. A time when all nations may be blessed. (Genesis XII 3, Psalm LXXII II). Thus the Hebrew nation of the Holy Land will be at the centre of the Kingdom (Exodus XIX 5-6, Micah IV 6-8 and Ezekiel XXXXII 21-28). The church universal of Abraham, yet of Christ, his descendant, central to our Godhead of Love as king, will reign in the New Jerusalem. (The Universal One Church of Love, AD2000, of the Godhead III.)

This then is the age of God's intervention through the supernatural. Cosmic Glory upon Earth.

("Ye shall seek me and find me, when you shall search for me with your heart.") Jeremiah 24, v 71.

"Many believed in Him because of the woman's testimony." John IV v 39

June Twilight in God's Garden of Love

(Late September 1989)

The Joyful evensong of our garden friends, dear Father, lifts high my soul to thee, dear Lord. One by one your feathered choristers cease their evening call to prayer. Twilight gives way to the golden silence and the mystery of night; revealing God is One of Love and Father over all.

The East where you were born and where you will come again in Glory no doubt? I was made aware of the vast distance, for You were revealed about eighteen inches in length (or height) transmitted from the Universe. This whole Revelation was in colour.

If Mary had ascended as with Christ our God of Love would have revealed her glorified, but this has not been revealed to us, so far? Perfect Love can only be that of Christ central to the loving three the soul of Christ was one with God, that Love of One in Three. The vision then retreated slowly, when over the Bibles a dark circular cavity opened in the corner of the wall and then retreated to the three cross site, and so returned to God in Glory, across the three cross site, †, T, +, close by our Chapel of Christ and our Father of Love.

One Light, One Love, One Church, of Three in Unity.

"Then they will see the Son of man coming in the clouds with great Power and Glory!" (Mark 13, v 26).

This then was the first occasion when our Godhead of Love confirmed that the visions were being sent down from Heaven to the three cross site and directed into our bedroom through the walls of our home (Amazing Grace).

Late October 1981

One evening, this month Beth was speaking of her visit to Brighton that day to see her sister M. They had been discussing their recent sad loss of their brother Paul and how the Son of their cousin's wife A, who had helped to nurse Paul had been given a Bible concordance from Paul's bequests. A's Son was currently living in Northern Ireland she said and perhaps it would help him? Beth was explaining this to me, and at the same time was sitting in the armchair by the fireside looking out on to our terrace at the southern end of our home. The terrace was bathed in a warm light and she had assumed that the light in the old stone wall was switched on? Suddenly there was a flash past the window and the light vanished! I then got up to switch on the light when she explained that this was a different light from that just revealed. The table could now be seen and canvas chairs, but that she had only seen the stone wall and garden plants and paving. I replied that she had most likely experienced the spiritual light (of Healing) and most likely would have experiences of the soul from now on? For the old stone wall I understood came from Holy Cross church after it was rebuilt many years ago. It was then used on a farm for a reconstructed stable I believe? When this was demolished I was able to purchase it for the walls at the south end of our new home.

November 1981

On the evening of the 21st November Beth was in the bathroom preparing for a visit to a Guides Party in their Hall, just down the road, of pilgrim's past. Then she opened the window to let the steam escape and was arrested in her thoughts when she saw the dead blooms of a bush of hydrangea below by the path full of white roses of the Light. She sensed great Joy and went into the bedroom and held the curtain over her head to blot out any background light. Once again the bush could be seen ablaze with many white roses of healing and she heard Heavenly church bells ringing. She experienced great Joy and it was a very happy party in the Girl Guides Hall that evening. Later I painted the impression of this small bush of white roses, seen below our bedroom window of the Divine visions from Heaven (many in fact).

Thus, in silence we rise up again, renewed through Love as one in Him, who Loves us all as One. For in Love our souls are Christed, made Eternally One in Him and He in us. One Godhead overall of Love, Truth, Power and Glory – Eternal Unity.

Just one experience here will never fade, for in His Love you will wish to return again and again to this link with Him as One. His garden-home of trees, lawns and three living tress, as of Calvary. Life is renewed here through His Eternal Love for all life, all Creation. Three arms of an old apple tree beckon you to a well of living water to the centre of this garden of Love, where bird-song compels you to sit and dream beneath a spreading Cedar and observe five arches of hazelnut, linked as One, the five senses of man, the five wounds of Christ. And if redeemed through Love you will find five gifts of the spirit. These arches linked as One, reveal the bridge of Loveform east to west, facing north to south to come, One church of loving Unity.

Peace reigns here where Love is perfected through faith and hope. Faith perfected through Hope and Love and Truth, doing His will in His Eternal One church. This is a site of spiritual Power and three-fold Glory.

Of Love, in which Christ and the Father reign as One: Here you will walk hand in hand with Jesus and the Father in humility and Glory and Peace, which flows ever-downward from the risen Cosmic centre of Glory and Love, for here dew, like manna from Heaven, distils all fear, in silent prayer you will discover the light of "I in Him and He in me (us)". God spoke to my soul one night. "The stable is to be called the chapel of Christ and the Father of Love". The Godhead III. One Church of Healing Love and Unity of III to come.

One Universal Church of Love

Our small stable runs east to west built by the former owner of this Holy Acre farm.

Isaiah 9, v 1

"The people that walked in darkness have seen a great light: they that dwelt in the land of the shadow of death, upon them has the light shined. Thanks be to our Godhead of Love." Isaiah thus foretold this age. The end of 2000 years of Christ and the dawn of the third millennium the Godhead III? (Thanks be to the amazing Love of our Godhead III in Unity, I cry out!)

Holy Acre † T

The Godhead of Love (November 1981)

At the end of each Lovely day my soul now sings to thee, dear Lord, friend and Brother, Father of all mankind and life. I see your reflected Love in each flower of spring, summer, autumn and winter here, a Love which speaks of Truth reborn each year of Freedom, Peace and Unity. Your garden-home of life renewed again, reborn of Love.

Here, my friends, we are surrounded with His light of Love, each hour, each day, each month of every year. A Love which speaks and sings and sighs with every breath of wind. No day dawns without your Song-birds' call to prayer, and later, evensong, at the end of each day. No day dies without the radiant Son of Light shedding new life upon us all throughout the Earth and Universe. For your Heavenly cross of north to south, east to west, is One of Unity.

Your lawns and fields which surround us are ever green, like the pine and cedar trees of old. All other trees of radiant summer glow have now shed their garments of many colours which for a season, return to Mother Earth from which they grew.

These three messages to my soul were granted during the twenty-one years of Baptist Bible teaching services.

("For whoever sees the Son, and believes in Him has life and I will raise him up at the last day." John 6, v 40).

Thanks be to our Godhead of Love, everlasting.

A Pilgrimage of Unity and Renewal (August 1981)

(September 1981-May 1982 – Revelations of Male/Female Priests

A happy band of pilgrims set out from Selsey, W. Sussex, on a mid-August morn, 1981, to commemorate St Wilfred's ministry, for St Wilfred brought the word of Truth to Sussex 1300 years ago (landing at Selsey Bill). For now at this time, during ten days of walking His churches were visited for prayer and sacrament, led by young men and women pilgrims, singing hymns and Songs of Love. And the hedgerows and woodlands echoed with their Joyful Love Songs, and the pilgrims daily, enjoyed the Bird Songs along the pilgrims way.

Daily the number of pilgrims grew and grew. The sun smiled upon them all journeying along many footpaths and bridleways as before, in centuries past, as with the pilgrims of old. For Sussex they say, was enshrouded in woodlands, the last county in England to proclaim, "The Way, the Truth and the Life." The pilgrim walkers were chiefly Catholics and a few Anglicans I believe?

At night on the evening before this pilgrimage began, for the third time, God sent us a vision of two priests and a kneeling worshipper dressed as a pilgrim of medieval times. One priest held out a chalice (cup of his passion) to the communicant, a loving woman, and the other priest, a woman, was reading the Word, and standing to the right, a few yards away, speaking and touching three lines of the Word of Life. Three of us joined this pilgrimage, for one day of great Joy, visiting God's houses of prayer. During the morning on the last day from Selsey many cabbage white butterflies flew over trees and hedgerows into God's garden here. In large numbers from the north, south, east and west – one for each pilgrim journeying to Rye I thought. God's amazing Love.

Over the next eight months God sent this vision of a male/female priest again and again: but in the ninth month, the 12 May 1982 (the ninth vision of three). Our loving Godhead revealed His mystical message of Love. 'The two are one' for the priests were now standing side by side, in the Unity of three, with the communicant to the left, kneeling as before. This person was dressed in an old leather coat and wearing ancient leather boots having large metal studs on the soles. A thirteenth century pilgrim no doubt! On this occasion, one priest was reading the Word, the assistant priest, a woman. The male priest held the paten (plate of bread, His body broken) from which shot upwards to Heaven, the Light.

Two rays of light as of the 'V' living bread of life, and light and Truth. The communicant with head bowed, awaited the one gift of bread of life, of Love from Christ and Our Father of Love, of word and sacrament in Unity. So as the spirit embraces the physical man or woman, so also the physical man or woman grows through the spirit of Truth. For the two are one in the Unity of Love, Christ indwelling in mind heart and soul.

In this scene, Christ of the Loving Godhead revealed that grace received through the word is co-equal to grace received through the Lord's supper (mass or communion), for the two are One in the glorious Godhead of three, of "I in Him and He in me the light of Love" is born anew. His words, "Do this in remembrance of Me", are words of Love of past, present and life to come, soul travel to Eternity.

Their Shrouds of life as food to the sleeping earth from whence they came. To see God in all Creation is to walk upon the face of the earth, hand in hand with Jesus, Lord of all.

We look forward to new life again of spring and summer days, of morning call of skylark, thrush and blackbird. For a season now the small birds reign supreme. The blue-tit, black-cap, finches, wrens and robins and the shy hedge-sparrow now greet us at daybreak, each morning, with their Songs of praise. The Godhead reigns over all the earth, for the Heavens were made by God for God the Son. And

God's word the Holy Bible is the book of Revelations. 'I am the One church the One world in the One Universe' is God's call to all.

We live in God's world for we are surrounded with his birds, and all life, and animals, plants and trees. His beauty of holiness, his flowers, colour, trees and Creation of light and life, reveal this beauty and is manifested in physical form to delight the soul, for with our spiritual eye He is One God of Love. With our hearts we understand this Love of Christ within, to Love our neighbours as One. With our souls we come to the knowledge of Truth. That the visible and invisible things of God from the beginning of time were designed to bring us to Him through Love, to His One Eternal church of Love and Unity, the Godhead III.

("You will rebuild the ancient ruins... restorer of ruined houses." Isaiah 58, v 12).

Thus God speaks to us through his word of life of testaments, Old and New: Love is His key.

Dear God, Your Church of Love is One (December 1982)

Love which came down at Christmas nearly 2000 years ago is born again each early Easter morn. Love which surrounds us now is one, One loving Father, Son and Holy spirit. One church of the Unity of Love in Three. The Godhead of Love Eternal.

Love is One church of life, revealed here in God's garden-home: Love renewed through your Godhead cross implanted on your garden Lord, facing east, close by a stable door. One centre of Love of the Inspired, Prophetic, and Revealed word of Truth. One church of Love Eternal. Our Godhead Divine reigns in Glory.

Love sends the angels, birds and butterflies revealing freedom of the spirit, as messengers of light, some by day, and some by night, they come, for Love transcends the law. Into God's garden home they fly, revealing Christ and Father are One. One Divine centre of life and light throughout the Universe linked to earth as one. One church of Love in Unity, the Godhead III.

Love transcends all life, for Love is of the Unity of all Creation and the word revealed. Love is one of Heaven on earth, for the Latin and Tau clover cross speak of the Unity of the Godhead as One, for the Heavens were made by God for God the Son, who calls to all: "I am the One church, in the One world, in the One Universe."

The Godhead of all Power and Glory.

Love spoke to my mind, heart, and soul many years ago in three sermons – over a period of twenty-one years of teaching in a branch of the Baptist Church: for during this period we shared worship with Anglicans and maintained fellowship with the Focolare RC movement and the Anglican Church in our parish.

1. "The Lord hath need of thee."
2. "I have no knowledge except that which is revealed to me."
3. "My Grace is sufficient for thee."

Next morning:

Bending low, I touched the now dew-sprinkled leaves of trefoil clover, upon which you placed a Latin cross of twigs pointing to the east in mid-June just five years ago. Now you confirm that day with a cosmic clover and grass (Tau) cross 'T' of Love, Joy, hope and Peace upon your garden home where you dear Father and Son, have appeared as One Church of Light, Eternal Love, and Unity of three. Later on the arm of the 'T' grew into the shape of Ireland, the other two into the shape of England, Scotland and Wales, finally one large green circle over six weeks to come, was revealed, of trefoil clover and grass.

As the last note of the unseen blackbird dies away, a pair of nocturnal bats, watchmen of the night, mount guard. Encircling your garden, trefoil cross and lawn they nightly watch, feeding as they fly, beneath the embracing branches of a mighty oak; Heavenly observers of the cross, they fulfil God's command.

Jesus Christ Father of Love, twice you came to us in your garden home, just as the 'Angelus' of parish bells rang out I bowed my head in your prayer of Love at the foot of the cross, filled with light Divine, when a mystical vapour of light and warmth spiralled up to Heaven from the earth. Your centre of the cross of Light now surrounds our home where God is One. An intersection point linking east and west and both north and south of our United Kingdom island home and all nations to come. Day surrenders to night, under a canopy of silent cosmic lights (the single eye and silent witness). For the three crosses are one.

Set in a sky of immeasurable height and light Eternal. Beauty claims our thoughts and life as Christ enters in; for all is silent now as your light Divine fills us with Love. The Glory of the light Universal transcends the night for the cosmic Cross and Church on earth are ever one. One Godhead, supreme overall.

As the choir boys ring, the church bells sing, 'One church of Love in Unity.'

Jesus of our loving Godhead, you sent us a message from your Divine centre of Love through your cosmic Latin and Tau cross on earth, that "The east will first link with the west, then the north with the south" (encircling the whole world and Universe). Unity of Love, one risen church of Love, embracing all.

There have been six messages to my soul on this Holy Cross Acre. One was after meditating on the recent death of a man in N. Ireland: "The Protestants' minds are filled with the knowledge of the word, the Catholics with the knowledge of the Saints." A Divine challenge from God to attend each other's form of worship, and to work and pray for loving Unity through loving our neighbours as one.

(From the minor prophet Amos 3, v 7. "Surely the Lord God does nothing without revealing his secret to his servants the prophets.")

Luke IV v 24

And He went on, "I tell you solemnly no prophet is ever recognised in his own country." A lifetime of searching for Reality. For such has been my experience now for over sixty years. Since God first spoke to my soul at the age of four in Devon, "Stand up for Truth and Justice," when I was staying with my grandparents at Kinders farm, Devon, for a few weeks in the autumn 1920.

One Son, One Well of Love, One Centre of Light

Two crosses † T intersection three ley lines, (June 81), and one ancient well

This is His garden-home, my friend, this is the stable, where Love calls you to come inside and pray. Here in silence He will come to you, my friend, in Love, for the Father and the Son are one. Cast all your pain, sickness, trials and care here as you kneel at the foot of God's cosmic cross, where you may pray in the silence of being 'One in Him, Lord of All'.

Beth planted this Christmas rose, and only nature can truly acknowledge these Heavenly gifts and does so in such a way that man (if he tries to analyse) is cut down to size, relative only to true appreciation and understanding that God alone is Sovereign, only that which is Truth enables freedom of Soul-growth. The all-glorious Godhead of all true Revelations is One.

(Before my Father died, early in 1961, one morning I recall, withdrawing the bedroom curtains in our home, Uckfield, Sussex. The rising radial arc of golden sunlight burst through the branches of the tree trunk on Birds-Eye Hill, and I stood transfixed. Blinded by God's light so freely given to all. Transfixed by this Glory, tears rolled down my cheeks and I understood some days later when my dear Father died suddenly. Nature worship is but a shadow of reality of the oneness of the all glorious Godhead III.)

The prayer of the farmer and gardener is one when they kneel on the soil to eradicate an obnoxious weed. We live from the products of the earth, and when we die the earth gives us a home prepared by the Creator and all provider. Nature's moods each season are reflective and like God reveals her priceless treasures if only we persist in our quest of Discovery? Only the heart discerns, the soul embraces, for only One God of Creation could produce such a blinding array of beauty. A scene of immense Love and beauty much as prophesied by St John the Divine? (For in wildness lies the preservation of the world and the loving Unity of all mankind. For my Son's bedroom looks out to our garden and the sites of where three butterflies revealed the Glory of God.

1. A Peacock resting on a white open flower (Love).
2. A Tortoiseshell, the symbol of Unity.
3. A Red Admiral – Freedom and the Glory of the Godhead III.

The skylark hovering high in the Heavens, and the morning chorus of the hedgerows, all breathing the pure early morning air of the countryside praise God in all His Glory with far more vigour than any mere person or child could ever possibly achieve. A closer observation would reveal that many of the tall dew-drenched grasses wreathed with pollen-laden seed-heads would be jostling with the brightly glowing herbs and weeds. What mind could contemplate this mystical and all glorious revelation? The tall slender meadow and fescue grasses were so gracefully arched, bending under the weight of the close set clusters of rounded seed heads, resembled hazelnuts to be discovered later in the hedgerows of the autumn season. ...And so the whole of the tensioned spider webs could also be seen linked to the taller weeds such as... docks, buttercups, foxgloves, horse (oxeye) daises, the rich deep yellow ragwort and Dresden blue flowered chicory stalks by the hedgerows.

Together with the herbs, each plant was thus linked in a united network throughout the whole field by many, many miles of silken threads woven all over the living herbage which now, though slowly at first, shed their priceless pearls of dew for the increasing diamond-like light warmth. For the sun's rays claimed their liquid bodies together with the rising temperature and invisible breeze. Nature is a complex web of life and man is an integral part of that web; unless freed by the Holy Spirit. The hand of God truly embraces the whole Universe and there is a sense of freedom overall, and that freedom is Love and wherever we may be, "Yes! I cry, God and his Son Jesus are One."

In the Hay-field, with a jerk of the reins, Prince and Duke drawing the solid iron wheeled mower, would leap into action. The carter (horse-driver) sitting on a central iron seat would guide his team, harnessed with flashing brasses, (and a single bell set at the top of each bridle) we both followed the working carter around the field over and over and over again, on all four sides, in fact, all day long. Sometimes having grown tired, one or both of us would fall asleep in the newly mown grass.

Pictorial beauty, wreathed in white May blossoms (hawthorn) perfumed pink and white and yellow honeysuckle, pale pink crab apple blossoms, the wild sloe, together with heavy sprays of elderberry. With the sun climbing higher and higher the whole field became enveloped in a golden haze of shimmering light. All day long many hundreds of colourful butterflies would fly out the of pathway of the approaching horses and move to the centre of the surrounding countryside never ceased to reflect the beauty, a butterfly on the wing caught by the sunlight to the dark tomb of a cocoon. We all need to experience mysteries in order to grow, for it is in stillness, silence, meditation, beauty and suffering God comes to us. The Bible, the inspired word, the Bible, the prophetic word, the Bible, the revealed word (Unity of the Godhead of three), the Bible, the word of Truth and mystery, the Bible, the revealed discovery and the word of Love, the Bible, the passage of life. For many years now God has sent the wild geese from the east and the seagulls from the west revealing bird flight phenomena, God the Divine Power over all freedom linking all life on earth to Heaven, the Divine centre of cosmic freedom God in Glory.

The bird Song of dawn and sunset echo the angels of Heaven, Love embraces all things for in Him is all life. There is a human birth, there is a spiritual birth, and there is a spiritual rebirth (soul) leading to the cycle of soul awareness and soul growth, in the totality of Love, through soul travel. Growth of "in the beginning was God" in the present is God, in the future God is. In my early youth, God spoke to me I sensed through the eyes? Now I see, hear, touch, smell and taste the Joy of Love. Also at the age of four God spoke to my soul, "Stand up for Truth and Justice."

The greatest gift is Love and an enquiring mind which can lead us into all mysteries, all Truths, Truth beyond religious beliefs to 'soul travel' and true reality of Creation. Of past, present and future – God within (the Light) and God without, the light of Eternity. The totality of life can only be experienced through consciousness (true self) yet is part of universal consciousness for it is with "He in us and we in Him" that we experience true freedom, for Truth (Love) alone sets us free. In the freedom of soul travel God takes us to the plane of all saints who individually or collectively through God the Son and Father lead us to that higher plane. That home of many passages through many mansions to the throne of total Love and all grace: the Divine centre of universal Love and Unity of Glory.

(In December 1982) God sent a vision of a young lamb walking along the top of a single wire fence. On the far side were two dead and tortured lambs and one asleep with a wolf-like dog crouching between them looking up to the Lamb of God. Here was a scene of Christ and the ever growing anti-Christian in our midst and of sacrifice to come? Repentance renewal = revelation was the call of three R's to all.

Predestination

As a child my first awareness of consciousness was through the passage of an enquiring mind. Growth of body with the mind, from the mind to heart, consciousness, to reality and finally Eternity. Thus predestination embraces God before, God in the present, God in the future, who is the One light of Love for the soul belongs to God through Love. Only with the indwelling of Christ (in mind, heart and soul) in spirit and nature can there be soul-growth, for of ourselves we can do nothing. Only God can feed our souls with Truth, via mind and heart to soul, of through Christ to God overall. I was born with a desire to discover both sides of Caesar's coin of Truth and Justice. Through a lifetime of seeking both, being called at the age of four the former, God's Truth, has been revealed. At the age of twenty-four, in 1940, on meditating on the death of a relative, I experienced Weald travel revealing the county of Sussex above the Weald, and downlands and the seashore of Sussex. At twenty-one in the army an experience of the Hand of God, protective and saving on a minefield. The experience of soul travel was so great a mystery that I kept silent until attending a Bible study group at the home of Baptists some fifteen to twenty years later, in our parish of Uckfield.

The greatest experience was to have witnessed (in a trance) on 17/18th July 1976, Christ's Head wrapped in the Holy Shroud napkin of the tomb (the light of Glory of Jesus, for two hours!) (baptism of death and new life, of Peace in Christ) and the all glorious Godhead vision (one of four) in the supper chamber at 5 a.m. on Easter morn 1978. Over twelve months of the risen radiant Lord, central to ten Disciples (resurrection of the cross of Love) in the One universal Church within the outline of a large human head, the Godhead III of Love. This was the scene of Easter evening from Holy scripture.

The Glory of freedom of the soul. Now I can recall those all-glorious Revelations to my soul for the soul belongs to God.

For all day long the gentle breezes from the east fanned the many intoxicating perfumes over the whole field of growing and newly mown grass. In the hedgerows the wild bumblebees, wasps, flies and honeybees filled the air with the rhythmic beatings of their tiny wings as the freshly opened wild flowers responded to the kisses of the sun. Together with their neighbours, the butterflies, they all expressed the freedom of their Creator, One God of Love in Unity.

For a brief while (one whole day) our all glorious Godhead thus lifted the dark shield of earthly sin to reveal the vision Shroud of Heavenly Truth and Glory, life and freedom, of the Eternal Love of both the Father and Son of all Creation, for all is Love in Unity.

(Christ said, "I am the bread of life, he that cometh to me shall never hunger." John 6, v 35.)

"One thing I do: forgetting what is behind and straining towards what is ahead, I press on towards the goal to win the prize for which God has called me Heavenwards in Christ Jesus." (St Paul Philippians 3, v 13-14).

Thanks be to God! I cry.

In one of the earliest visions our Lord was shown standing in the shadow of a tree and held in his hand a pottery bowl into which the woman of Sychar, Samaria, was pouring water. Suddenly the water pot turned to a golden glow revealing the living presence of our Lord.

And there followed Jesus' promise, "I can only give you the living water of life."

I am grateful to all those writers and teachers (especially of the Bible) who have either confirmed or contributed to my thought pattern, to writings, to consciousness, to experiences, to the fuller awareness of 'Eternal Love'. What are we except that we are mindful of God the source of all life, all Creation, all Truth, all Beauty, the One church of Love, woven in the book of Love and Truth, the Bible. There are a few perhaps who truly Love the Bible with mind heart and soul. The cross of Jesus, the cup of his passion of water and wine, the plate of broken bread, His body, yet in these three elements, and the word lies the Power through faith. The Power is One in the pure Love of Jesus' cross leading us to the Eternal church of Love of the risen cross of both the Son and Father of the loving Godhead of Universal Glory. Love that is within this world but not of this world, but of total Universal Power. As Paul said, "The kingdom of God is not in word but in Power." The Power of Unity of our Lord's supper and the word is One, revealed through the wisdom of God. The first church of the Godhead today has so many branches: Renewal and Intersection and pruning branches will lead to a New Church founded wholly on Truth and Love. Born again in Unity, for did not Jesus say, "I am the vine, ye are the Branches." Jesus foretelling this age of growing Unity of Love.

Truth is revealed knowledge of Creation, Word and Spirit. The Creation and the Word came first, then with our Lord's three years of ministry (teaching and healing) he instituted the Lord's Supper (the one Last Supper) then together with the Father founded the One church of Love. The word (Truth revealed) for in it is concealed the light of Revelation and Salvation through Love, of both the Father and Son, one of Eternity, One church of Love. The risen cross of Glory ever shines linking our souls as One in Him in soul travel to the throne of all Glory and Creation. Jesus said, "Except a man be born again, he cannot enter the Kingdom of God!" Hence 'soul travel' is of the Glory of God.

Of Fatima, Portugal (1917)

Saturday 28th November 1981

This evening before going to sleep I read two or three chapters of *The True Glory Of Fatima*. The experiences of the children of Fatima were read after reading the Bible. From the chapter concerning the visitation of the Virgin Mary to three children, the lady opened the palms of her hands to reveal to them a scene of the world of the devil.

(Reported in 1981-March 1982)

At night, having prayed Our Lord's Prayer, being filled with the Holy Spirit, I was in darkness yet aware of a small circle of spiritual light appearing over the Fatima publication and three Bibles at my bedside. It quickly developed into a human form on my right. This form, magnified, was of a beautiful woman. The luminous marble-like figure of Mary with baby John the Baptist (unclothed) sitting on her left knee holding high a Latin cross pointing to the Heavens over her right shoulder. Mary was smiling at John, yet was looking beyond to perhaps her own child (God's Son) Jesus on the floor? A scene of exquisite beauty and Love not to be found in this world except that it be granted through the Divine Power overall, our Godhead of Love. (This I feel was Mary's visit to her cousin Elizabeth?)

The vision then changed to a spherical light and retreated through the wall which suddenly opened to form a circular cavity, and so, returning to the cosmic clover Tau and Latin cross site on our garden lawn, and so to the Divine centre of the Godhead Universe, overall, of Universal Power and Glory. Often in life I have prayed to know and to do the Lord's will. (This revelation of the Divine Godhead from whom we have been granted signs of light Eternal.) Thus I have been made aware of the earth linked with the Divine Creator?

I then fell asleep after speaking of it to Beth who was at my side, in bed. During the night filled with the spirit there appeared a vision over the three Bibles on the shelf on my right and the book of Fatima, revealing a magnified red creature with outstretched wings and long gaping mouth full of savage teeth. It reminded me of a pterodactyl or pteranodont and was I feel, 'the creature', Dragon, or the devil shown to the three children in the palms of the hands of Mary of Fatima? For I had read that it was after the third visit of the Lady to the three children that they also experienced in the open, near a tree, and subsequent visits on the 13th day of each month from May to October 1917.

Thirteen I have grown to recognise as a mystical number in my life, yet the three, daily, transcends all, for in the three and the multiple of the three is the greatest of all Divine mysteries, the oneness of our Godhead III.

March/April 1982

On the opposite side of the brick path, under the wall and below our bedroom window of visions, and close to the Hydrangea bush, a single Christmas Rose plant suddenly began growing at an excessive rate and over some six weeks to two months produced well over a hundred blooms which Beth was able to pick and take out to sick friends in our parish. The stems grew to a height of six to nine inches tall. Beth carried Christmas Roses in her bouquet on our wedding day, December 22nd, 1948. My sister, M, who died a few years ago gave me the plant, twelve months before dying (one of three healthy plants).

(From John 3, v 2)

"Beloved, now we are the children of God, and it has not been revealed what we shall be but we know that when He is revealed we shall be like Him for we shall see Him as He is."

South of our home is a Lombardy poplar. Today a pigeon flew out of the oak tree near the stable and following the heron overhead it also settled, but on a lower branch of the holly tree (passion of our Lord). Only yesterday my eldest grandchild, M, came to borrow an illustrated book on birds. Nearly seven years ago, just before her sister, A, was born, early that Sunday morn, she ran into Beth's bedroom in the morning and called out, "The geese, the geese." An hour and a half later I set out for a service in Holy Cross Church when I noted two 'V' formations of geese flying from west to east! M and I were both granted foreknowledge that her sister to come, born four to five hours later, was to be a girl! Two of a kind: the wild geese were also sacred to the Druids in Deity worship I believe?

Truth and the Divine Power

June 1982

The American poet, writer, and philosopher, Wealden Thoreau, had this to say concerning Truth, "If a man does not keep pace with his companions perhaps it is because he hears a different drummer. Let him step to the music that he hears, however measured or far away."

Yes – have the courage to seek the Truth, to practise the Truth. To follow the Truth, when one day Truth will set you free. Truth is man's spirit liberated like the first Brimstone butterfly which never fails to appear early each spring morn. On a warm March day or in the early April sunshine, (Truth is in fact soul revelation the gift of God) what Joy this first sighting gives us as with the first shy snowdrop or primrose of each early spring. God never fails to send signs of his presence, transcending all those of man.

Follow the inner light of single-mindedness (soul) but first shed the Shroud of self-will. His will is Love, which is the way, the Truth, and the Life.

Real life demands courage, steadfastness, and willingness to face loneliness, poverty, and persecution along life's road of soul-growth and travel. The fruits are Love, Joy, Hope and Peace Eternal. Born on the wings of Love, light as the thistledown of high summer, set free by goldfinches feeding. Like umbrellas of light they are carried ever upwards by the wind of the spirit a most glorious experience found. Manifestation of the beauty of life is indeed an experience of Joy, such as the summer opening of a pure white rose, growing by an old apple tree here in the centre of God's garden. Things of the earth are in time, but things of the spirit are timeless. The marriage of the soul with the Hand of Heaven is like a priceless pearl or a single droplet of dew shining on a velvety petal of a pure white rose on a June morning. Something happens when a ray of light of the new born sun strikes it and the liquid pearl responds by sending showers of radiant light forward and like the all radiant risen Christ born again of Easter morn. All is light and the soul grows through such experiences, One God, One World, One Universe, One Light Eternal. The Unity of Jesus and our Father God overall, The Godhead III.

From the Old Testament missionary and prophet Ezekiel we have chapter 12, v 24 "...the day is coming when every vision will come true..." (v 28) "...the vision that man sees concerns the distant future, he is prophesying for times far ahead."

("God never fails to give the Holy Spirit to those who ask." Luke 11, v 13)

("You believe because you can see Me. Happy are those who have not yet seen and yet believe." John 20, v 29).

Of Knock, Ireland (1975)

2nd February 1982

The visions of Joseph, Mary and St John the Evangelist are reported in 'The Cross and Glory' witnessed by about fifteen poor people of the village of Knock about one hundred years ago, seen at the gable end of the parish church one evening when fine rain, like dew, was falling upon the scene.

Having read the Bible and after a prayer I experienced spiritual possession when a very large magnified arm and hand (Hand of God) was projected through the east window of our bedroom. The hand slowly opened revealing three magnified persons standing in long light garments. These quickly faded when I was shown three heads so human-like, in quick succession. Firstly a clear and sharply defined bearded man (human-like) probably Joseph, secondary a woman of great beauty with dark hair, Mary? And thirdly a man, probably St John the Evangelist? All of human living form. Then our Lord revealed the three standing side by side above our bodies, as in the vision of Knock. All were magnified by the soul. A scene of Divine Love of Husband, Wife and Teacher. Unity of three and the Mother of our Lord of Light.

One Church of Love overall.

Since the trance and vision of our dear Lord's head in the napkin of the tomb experienced during the night of 17-18 July 1976, the Divine Godhead has granted us many visions, often on the eve of a saint's day, I have sensed?
Of the disciple, teaching, writing, preaching, working as the Apostles, One body in Christ, of Word and Sacrament of Love. The early Church of Love in Unity of the loving Father, of the loving Son and loving Holy Spirit, the Godhead III overall.

("May they be so completely one that the world will believe that it was You who sent Me." John 17, v12)

("The creature itself also shall be delivered from the bondage of corruption into the glorious liberty of the children of God." Romans VIII, v 21)

("God's elect; strangers in the world of man?" Peter 1:1 NIV Bible.)

The Cross with all its Shame and the Cross of Glory are One with the Godhead of Love

(June 1982)

Twice this summer our loving Godhead has sent us visions of Christ on the Cross of Calvary. Both of these experiences were brief revelations of the suffering of our dear Lord who died for us all on God's tree of life. Only the spirit can lead us into all Truth; that is, the two are one, the redeeming cross of Love of almost 2000 years ago, of now and into eternity. For God's Love is Christ's Love so freely given to us all. One Light, one Love of the all glorious Godhead III.

My spiritual life has developed through the sacraments (Anglican teaching) and the Word of Baptist teaching, and of the prophecy, and the gospels of Love and as taught by the Focolare of the (Catholic) Church. For all three over some twenty-one years contributed to the deepening of our spiritual life, Beth and myself. For God spoke to my soul at the age of four when staying at my grandparents' farm 'Kinders' Devon, "Stand up for Truth and Justice." And so throughout life I have been searching for reality.

Grace revealed Christ on the cross of Calvary a few weeks ago, when our Lord called us to go on an Ecclesiastical pilgrimage from Arundel in West Sussex to Buckfast, Devon, the county of my birth.

His loving presence at night before departure, was then manifested through pressure applied twice to my legs. And for fourteen days he appeared daily, after mass or the Last Supper, revealing that the two are one, of Sacrament and Word. The word is necessary to daily living and the word is necessary to spiritual growth of Love, which is for the mind, heart and then the soul. Yet the soul we may discover belongs to God and is the Amazing Grace of God which revealed the Godhead III.

August 14th – 28th 1982

Love sent the spirit of Love about two weeks ago when the Peace which God had granted us was being challenged by the institutional church? Filled with the spirit an Angel of Light lifted me up bodily from our bed and pressed me to his breast. This is the Glory we may receive when our lives are activated for the Unity of Love, the Universal One church. Embraced by our Angel of the Lord of Universal Glory.

And so our Godhead of Love will continue to reveal the oneness of the church of Love, for we have no knowledge except that which is revealed to us, for revelation is total Love and is One.

From William Blake the poet, artist and visionary:

"All must Love the human form,
In heathen, Turk or Jew,
Where mercy, Love and pity dwell
There God is dwelling too."

Love is the word, Love is the spirit, Love is the Truth, Love is the Power, Love is the Glory.

"Beloved now we are children of God, and it has not been revealed what we shall be but we know that when He is revealed, we shall be like Him, for we shall see Him as He is." (1 John 3, v 2)

Thank God I cry.

"I was strengthened as the Hand of the Lord my God was upon me." (Ezra 2, v 28)

(Thanks be for his Amazing Grace and Eternal Glory Divine)

7th November 1982

Beth whilst attending a service was with the Cub Scouts in Holy Cross Parish Church on 7 November. This month, the curate the Revd. Simon Holland was preaching on the early church. Suddenly Beth noticed a light shaft of spiritual light shooting up to the roof from the water pipe of the heating system underneath the grating of the floor. It came out from a point in the pipe that branches out before the altar in the little Cardale Chapel on the south side of the Chancel. This was a soul revelation she noted that the water pipe glistened with light on the top of the pipe. This experience she said seemed to confirm that the cub scouts were like an underground church reaching out to all countries through God's two great commandments. To Love God and our neighbour as One. That water seemed to be the healing element she said.

The preacher-teacher had been speaking of experiences of the first early church – the call from God to *return to the Bible as the prime source of grace*, i.e. a Godhead revelation in fact.

On a previous occasion at the Lord's Supper (HC) I was kneeling at the altar rail with hands cupped awaiting God's gift of bread, of His body broken when I was filled with the Holy Spirit before the passing of the broken bread was placed into my cupped hand by the priest. This confirmed my faith of the Eternal presence of our loving Lord when Christians assemble in prayer and Love. This also was an experience in the Cardale Chapel of the Holy Cross church.

Over some twenty-one years of worship in Holy Cross I have frequently noted the top three arms of the crucifix by the lectern. In the priest's sermon when Bible reading, the cross would glow with spiritual light, but *never* the carved image of Jesus! Ever since the visitation of our Dear Lord here I am convinced that the simplicity of the cross, and the Bible, is more meaningful, unless the carver had been granted a vision before the execution of the crucifix?

The Light, God's light, continues to pour down from Heaven, the throne of all grace, Power and Glory. the church is once again challenged by the Holy spirit and word of Love, of Christ, of the loving Godhead calling us to a greater daily Unity, of Love in Him who Loves us all, for with the Godhead of all Love, Light and Truth the Power, is one of freedom. Just as Jesus was freed from the tomb, born again, so also may we be through Love. The call is for all branches of the 'One True Vine' to "return to the Bible as the prime source of grace"; Unity of Love.

God gives us life. God gives the soul, the spirit of freedom and Peace. God is present at Baptism and the Sacrament of Love giving us new life. God is present in renewal (following repentance) when we are reborn of Love, God surrounds us now with His light of all-glorious Revelation, when special Grace is received from high (except ye are born again) revelation. God grants us wisdom greater than the knowledge of any man or any form of institutional worship, for true Love embraces all.

God sent a message at the last visitation, to go on a pilgrimage to the West, on the seventh anniversary of the visitation of the cosmic Godhead cross, a Latin cross of hazel twigs on our lawn, by a stable door facing East. Our feeble earthly bodies are in time, yet our timeless souls belong to God who first gave them to us to feed with Love and to do His will. for with God there is no time: Love, Joy Hope and Peace are all gifts of the spirit. Yet they are passages in time through which we must travel seeking to do His will at all times and freedom, through Love, revealed. Before being changed by Him from Glory into Glory, into His likeness. Free as the wind in the cosmos or blowing across the face of the earth is the spirit in the world but not of this world, Love of the oneness and Unity of Christ and our Father God. For Love is the Spirit, Love is the Power, Love is the Glory.

One church of Love in Unity, the Godhead III, One church to come.

(This command of Jesus: "Be filled with His fullness" (Ephesians 1, v 17) "that the God of our Lord Jesus Christ, the Father of Glory, may give you the spirit of Wisdom and Revelation in the knowledge of Him.")

"Thanks be to God!" I cry. Amazing Grace.

Nightfall – Christmas 1982

O blessed light Eternal, Dear God Shining throughout the Universe, please pour down from the vastness of your Creation your messengers of Love to embrace us all by night and day. Within your outstretched arms of Love enfold us, till the dawn watch shall once again call us, dear Saviour and guardian of our sleep, shine upon us all.

In the fullness of your Love and Peace Lord, let our souls become embraced through yours. For if, through Truth, our souls are Christed we become One in you, your light in us, Dear Saviour, Lord of all. Speak to us in the silent passage of soul travel, One with the soul and you, of Peace, of Love and Life Eternal, beyond the moon and stars.

Round us falls the night, the busy world, now hushed, grows dim, I see your Heaven ablaze with cosmic lights and your Advent star, of golden light revealed now proclaims your great Love, of life renewed (reborn) for out of this earthly Shroud of darkness bursts forth the Christmas message of Love, anew.

Of Christ reborn of Love renewed, "One church of Love." The bells on earth rejoice as the choirs of Heaven sing loud and clear. The Glory of the oneness of Christ and our Father of Love in Unity.

A Pathway to the God of Love
Seventy-eight Years of Travel

Searching for the Kingdom of Light
(From birth, 31 March 1916 to March 1986)

The greatest experience in the world is Discovery through Love, to see God in all things, God's hand in all Creation. A newly born child leads us to a stable, a fledgling on a lawn to a nest and home of intricate beauty.

The New church of Christ of the All glorious Godhead III, Unity, in a New Age of Love revealed, as predicted by one of the greatest teachers, Paul (disciple of our Lord's third millennium I feel).

"It is in Christ that the complete being of the Godhead dwells embodied, and in him you have been brought to completion. Every Power and authority in the Universe is subject to him as Head." (Colossians 2, v 9-10 NEB).

Thanks be to Jesus and the New Testament Prophets foretelling the third millennium I sense. Through Christ to God our Father of all.

The Risen Christ, One Church of Love

(Jan 9th-Feb 5th, 1983)

Jesus last night, filled with your Love, you claimed my soul with soul travel to the high rocks and tomb of Gethsemane. Risen and glorified by the Father of Love you suddenly burst through the upright massive flat stone on the face of the tomb. You being filled with radiant light of that Resurrection morn, born again of God. In your right hand you held the staff of life, the light prophesied by King David, in his psalm (23) of Love some 3000 years ago. From scripture (Matthew) reports that the stone was rolled away by the Archangel and this may have followed the resurrection scene as granted to my soul?

Lord, seven days later you sent us a vision of Jesus' walking staff of light in our bedroom when an unseen Angel stood by the Bibles on our right. This staff again appeared on the following night and from its centre burst forth the huge hand and arm of God pointing to the west, with the palm uppermost, projected from the east, and magnified by the soul.

Several times larger than human size, it was slowly withdrawn and instantly replaced by twenty arms and hands also facing upwards, thus creating an arc to the north, to the west, and the south. These we believe were the hands and arms of your loving ten Disciples in the supper room awaiting your return, new life from the tomb, to go forth into the whole world and preach the word of life to all mankind and to heal, (perhaps this vision also indicated the growth of Unity to come with the Jews) in the Western half of the world, to be concerned for the freedom and Unity of all people and for helping to feed all those countries in need (the third world). For God said, "The east shall first link with the west, and then the north with the south," here by the three cross site. Thus the Western nations are called to help the Eastern half of the world (God's message calls for Unity from the three cross site here by our stable, 15 June 1975-15 June 1987.

Once again our Godhead of Love calls to us all as One to heal the many divisions in his One church Love to do his Will, to rise, stand up, as pilgrims of old, and preach and practise the Gospel of Love and Truth throughout the whole wide world and Universe. To spread the good news, and heal the sick, through you dear Lord who by your sacrifice and life renewed grants to us all the wholeness, and the oneness of your One church of Love, the Godhead III.

Isaiah that great prophet in 740BC prepared us for this New Age so long ago. "All day long I have stretched out my hands to a disobedient and contrary people." (Was this not also a prediction of our dear Lord's hands and arms nailed to the cross? 2000 years ago, and in the Resurrection supper chamber, the experience of the glorious Godhead III, Easter morn, 1978).

Last Sunday night, the 31st January, the spirit of Love in a vision revealed a small square table spread, with a bottle central, (one sacrifice?) and on the right was a lady priest holding an open Bible, we doubt reading or teaching?

With the forefinger of her right hand she pointed to three lines of scripture, teaching an unseen assembly, called of God. A scene of the early Church? Calling us all to evangelise, and so foretold to heal divisions through the Unity of Love, our greatest gift of all from our Godhead III of Love.

Seeing God, Hearing God, Touching God, Smelling God of Creation and Tasting God is Love

The Godhead III (9th March 1983)

Yesterday I saw you in your garden God, central in a bed of bright purple heather, then I heard you call as your busy bees flew in and out gathering nectar for their winter store from the bosom of each new blossoming flower kissed by the morning sun. Out of the centre of this Heavenly scene flew this season's first messenger of light, a golden Comma butterfly, emerging from its winter home reborn of warmth, of Love, of Light and Truth.

Bending low I sensed your loving touch Lord as I gathered three pure white snowdrops of virgin birth, for with each scene and scent, of recurring spring, dear Lord, you send your messengers of Light and Love to remind us that your great sacrifice was Love for everyone, all life, the one Godhead over all.

With white heads bowed of petals three, they shyly revealed three chalices of green, containing central a taste of the nectar of life, renewed, each year. No other flower speaks so silently of your sacrifice dear Lord of humility, and purity of Love reborn in this year of 1983, (divisible by three) of the oneness of the inspired, prophetic and revealed word of Love the Bible. With your mystic touches of Love I have also seen signs in your lawn of a triangle of grasses and clover (over an ancient well). A dark circle of green grass, woven as a circle, revealing the Unity of the Power of Love to heal the Godhead III. On another occasion the green cross of St Andrew appeared in this green grass circle, over the well. For beneath this scene there lies an ancient stream of living water of God. (The Queen Mother had returned from her holiday in Scotland the day before the cross appeared.)

God speaks to us from the Gospels as one to the heart and soul of Testaments Old and New, of the Godhead overall, in the still small voice in the silence of night I have grown to Love. With each visitation of angels of light I sense your presence near, Dear God, is one of Truth supreme, for the revealed word of life is light for all throughout the world, and Universe, your church is one.

God speaks to us through wisdom for at the end of each day, as night time falls, I read your 'word of life' and pray. On extinguishing the bedside light I see your continuing light in the Heavens, serving the whole wide world of God to man.

One God, One church of sovereign Love, overall is your Eternal call. And when I fall asleep you embrace and protect us enfolded in your Eternal Love overall. Your All-Seeing Eye keeps watch dear guardian of our souls, One Lord of Love.

("I will speak of the glorious honesty of thy majesty and of thy wondrous works." Psalm 145, v 5)

("The Lord is my light and my salvation, whom shall I fear." Psalm 27)

New Life in the New Church, in a New Age

(20th April 1983)

Embraced by Love, cradled by darkness yet having inward light, born of Love, born through Love to emerge, the light of the world. His light, his world of Love. (For did He not say, "I am that I am.")

Jesus said, "I am the light of the world, the Good shepherd, the BREAD of life the Wine of the vine, the One True Vine (Godhead). The way, the Truth and the Life." (His will.) For the body exists to feed the soul with Love and Truth, first to the mind, then the heart, then to the soul, for this latter belongs to God: One name, One sacrifice, One Church of Love. One Godhead overall.

Then Love is Unity, Love is Truth, Love is wisdom, Love is life reborn, Love can only be discovered through loving or suffering, can only be experienced and revealed through the Light, through Love of all Creation, for all life is His, through all citizens of the earth. Mother Julian discovered this light, His Love, his sacrifice for all, in May 1373 at Norwich, in the east of our beLoved country. (The following lines are from her 'Revelations of Love').

"I am the foundation of your praying", and it came to her: you would know the meaning of this thing? Love was his meaning, who showed it you? Love. Why did he show it? For Love. Hold on to this. This Light is Love, and its measuring is done to us by the wisdom of God. Thus Love keeps us in faith and hope, and faith and hope leads us into Love and at the end all shall be Love.

Six hundred years have since passed on, yet you dear Lord unceasingly as God ever continues, never fails to reveal your Love which is free and is one. For there is nothing which is hid which you cannot expose by the Light. One church of Love of freedom overall. God sent us a message with his three circles of seagulls on the 600th anniversary of Mother Julian's revelations. Three concentric circles of gulls appeared over our stable and the site of three crosses to come. God wants a new church founded on Love, reborn of Truth, the oneness of Creation, and the word Revealed. One church purified through the Godhead overall embracing the whole wide world, and the word of Love in Unity of all. Prophecy, "Abide in him, that when He shall appear we may have confidence." (John II, v 28).

Your Light within and without is One

(mid-June 1983)

When your (son) sun first shone upon your countryside and our home dear Lord I then knew you from your light within (soul). You my dear beLoved Father keeper of my soul from birth, through growth, have always beamed down your spiritual rays of Light and Love and Truth from the beginning of time, for all life is yours, and you are one in your most precious jewel, this earth, your island home, in your universal space of all Creation. This gem created by our Godhead of Love for all mankind, far surpasses all works of the world of man.

You gave me a free will to search through life to discover that Eternal life is one of Love of first "You in me and I in you" one Lord of Light and Father of all. Like a brilliant shaft of light by day you have so often appeared at night as of the Resurrection morn. One glorified body embracing all for out of the darkness of this world you shine within our souls the light of Love and Joy, life and Peace, in your Eternal Glory for the word and you are one of "Bread of life", and your wine, Food of Truth for mind, heart and soul.

Immortal undying is your cross of Love with arms ever extended we hear your Eternal call. "Come unto Me, forsake your former life (as with his Disciples) for it is with Love you renew us One Lord of Light overall! What we observe with the eye and all we hear with the ear, is it not our quest for Truth to feed the heart the haven of the soul? For our souls grow only through Love and Truth to freedom which you dear Father so freely gives to all, day by day, dear saviour of my soul."

One Light, One living church of Love in Unity.

("Abide in him that when he shall appear we may have confidence." John 2, v 26.)

("Everyone that is of the Truth heareth my voice." John 18, v 31).

"I am" (24th June 1983)

Isaiah that great prophet of old speaks of Eternal values of Unity when he says:

"Then shall thy light break forth as the morning and thine healing spring forth speedily, and thy righteousness shall go before thee: the Glory of the Lord shall be thy reward. Then shall thou call, and the Lord shall answer, thou shalt cry, and he shall say: 'Here I am.'" (58, v 8-9)

("Thanks be to God.")

How gloriously wonderful it is to experience the Truth through manifestations of the Divine word to the soul, as on the occasion when I stood on the lawn close by your stable here dear Lord (the site of the three cosmic crosses to come) after sighting overhead three concentric circles of seagulls flying from the west in mid-June 1973, and one circle in mid-February 1974. On the 600th anniversary of the Prophet, St Julian of Norwich (a huge screaming circle of gulls, clockwise form). Then our Lord God answered my call (in meditation, February 1974) in silence of the soul:

"I am the One church in the One world in the One Universe" (as I looked Heavenwards).

(The Silent Witness, the Hand of God, the All-seeing Eye, Jesus Lover of my soul.)

Surely God's message was simply, "The universal life of God," the Power to heal, and make all things new:

Freedom, Peace, Power and Glory and Unity.

Again and again our loving Godhead has revealed the oneness of Truth of our risen radiant Lord as in the four visions of the Godhead of the Supper Chamber – Christ central to His Loved ones, Christ risen central to the Godhead of all Truth, Glory and Life to come. (Two other revelations of our dear Lord at supper with his Loved ones have also been granted).

A poem composed by Father Andrew SDC speaks of my early childhood (Devon and East Sussex coasts, N-S, E-W) growth, and adulthood, as one revealed, throughout life:

I Love this Peaceful flat land
That stretches out to the sea
The cattle that slowly wander
The birds that cry noisily,
The shadows of clouds that pass,
The sedge and the pale strong grass,
And the fresh salt scent of the sea.

My soul feels a sense of welcome,
As of land familiar and known;
The solitude soothes me and tells
I am free, I have come to my own.
Dear God if I might be a hermit
'Tis here in contentment I'd be
With the wild birds above me
And my cell, and beyond it the sea.

(I hope I shall be forgiven for printing this? For I do not know the author or have his authority.)

The Godhead can only be fully experienced through repentance, renewal and revelation: the Freedom of Peace, of mind heart and soul, (New Age theology). John the Baptist was sent of God to proclaim Christ, a New Life, in a New Age, a new church for 2,000 years to come. So John calls today, again, calls to the whole world through Christ as one, in an age of preparation for a renewed life in Christ in the Godhead of Love, One church of Unity and freedom of the third millennium, for Jesus died for all, the Godhead III.

"John came into the wilderness and all the country about Jordan, preaching the baptism of repentance for the remission of sins." As it is written in the words of Isaiah, the prophet, saying, "The voice of one crying in the wilderness. Prepare ye the way of the Lord make his paths straight. Every valley shall be filled and every mountain and hill shall be brought low: and the crooked shall be made straight, and the rough ways shall be made smooth: and all flesh shall see the salvation of God." (Luke, 3 24).

This proclamation of John forecast a New church of the Loving Godhead (all flesh). Hence in this New Age we are to return to our roots, the founding of the first early church of the loving Godhead of the Word, of Baptism, and of the Lord's supper (Unity of three). We should remember that the apostles, as evangelists, carried old testament scriptures armed with the knowledge of Christ's three years of healing and Teaching and the Holy spirit of light was manifested in them. "Thy will be done."

Mother Julian of Norwich also proclaimed this 'New Age' (the Godhead third millennium) with the words:

"And all things shall be well, and all things shall be well, and all manner of things shall be well."

For these were the words which St Julian spoke to my soul, being first awakened by the Holy spirit at night, about seven days after we had arrived for a holiday with our Son C, in Hannover. This date was 18th September 1983.

A New Age, a new church, founded on the Oneness of the word of Truth and Light, of Faith and of the Godhead of Love, One well of living water of life which our loving God granted to the peoples of the old testament, one well of living water of life so freely granted to us all of the new through Christ of the Godhead overall, one well of life Eternal.

(On this occasion in Hannover, during the night the long pair of E window curtains were lifted up to the ceiling slowly by the unrevealed hands of God. A very cool circular motion of air when St Julian spoke to my soul, then they were slowly lowered at the end of her message).

Christ said, "Behold I make all things new," and has done so throughout two thousand years almost and will do so in the New Age. Confirmed in so many ways, as on the night when the spirit revealed three Bibles on our bedside table each ablaze with radiant light! It was the same light as that of the risen, radiant Christ granted through 'soul travel' Resurrection morn, (Easter day at 5 a.m. 1978) when our dear Lord risen from the tomb burst through the east wall of the supper chamber to comfort his anxiously awaiting Disciples. Truth and the Divine words of Love. (The Bibles were: Revised English Bible, the Jerusalem Bible, Catholic, and the King James Bible). Later when taking photocopies of this painted vision, two small white circles appeared on two Bibles linked together as one – the King James Bible and the Jerusalem RC. Unity to come?

With Him and in Him is the total light of Eternity, and this light is his Amazing Grace. All physical barriers are eliminated through our God of Love, an experience of the Eternal light.

Only through the practice of loving relationships with all peoples and our Godhead III may we experience the totality of Revelation: that Unity of Creation and the word made One through Love. Jesus's great commandment:

(For so the Lord has commanded us: "I have set you to be a light to the Gentiles, that you should be for salvation to the ends of the earth." Acts, 13, v 47.)

Luke IV 18-19 foretells:

"The spirit of the Lord has been given to me, for he has appointed me. He has sent me to bring the good news to the poor, to proclaim liberty to the captives and to the blind new sight, to set the downtrodden free, to proclaim the Lord's year of favour."

(Thanks be to our Godhead of Love.)

(I cry, for a few tears have rolled down from my eyes!)

The Godhead of Love

(Sunday 3rd July 1983)

Some sow while others reap. So it is with the preparation, planting and harvesting of crops, and so also it is with the spoken, written and revealed word of Love. There are some who Love and sow Love to living seeds, plants and animals, birds, and all life both great and small, others reap the harvest of this sowing.

The Godhead is pre-eminent in Creation and the Word, for the spirit is one revealing that both the Father and Son's Love is One of Unity, the Power to heal and make us all free. The hymn *How Great Thou Art* really captures this Unity of One God and One church of Love:

> "Oh Lord my God when I in awesome wonder
> consider all the works thy hand has made.
> I see the stars, I hear the mighty thunder
> Thy Power throughout the Universe displayed.
>
> (chorus)
> Then sings my soul, my saviour God to thee how great thou art.
>
> When through the woods and forest glades I wander
> and hear the birds sing sweetly in the trees
> when I look down from lofty mountain grandeur
> and hear the brook and feel the gentle breeze.
>
> (chorus)
>
> And when I think that God his Son not sparing
> sent Him to die I scarce can take it in,
> that on that cross my burden gladly bearing
> He bled and died to take away my sin.
>
> (chorus)
>
> When Christ shall come with shout of acclamation
> and take me home what Joy shall fill me heart
> when I shall bow in humble adoration
> and there proclaim my God how great thou art.
>
> (chorus)
> Then sings my soul, my saviour God to thee how great thou art.

(John 17, 23)

(Neither for these only do I pray, but for them also that believe on me through the word: that they may all be One, even as thou Father are in me and I in Thee that they also may be in us: that the world may believe that thou didst send me and Lovest them even as thou Lovest me.)

(This lovely early Russian hymn, above all others I feel relives experiences of my early childhood in the countryside and indeed God's revelations of the Glory of Creation throughout life).

Love – July 1983

The Unity of Love

One God of Love of testaments old and new.
One God of Love who makes all things new.
One God of Love who speaks to us through channels of grace.
One God of Love who answers prayer channels of Love.
One God who listens to our pleas from mind, heart and soul.
One God in Unity of three of word, baptism and supper of Love.
One God who Loves each child on earth.
One God who rejoices with each spiritual rebirth.
Made One in him and he in us, One Godhead overall.

With Love we Love and see Love.
With Love we hear Love and share Love with all.
With Love planted in Love we build Love.
With Love his Love touches us, and we see Love.
In Love with Love lies the Power to make all things new,
In Love with Love we may see His Light of Eternity.
In silence we listen to Love and God speaks to our souls.

In Love we rejoice for Love is timeless.
With Love we sing and glorify Love of threefold Power.
Love is not of this world but of the universal Godhead of Love III.
Made One in him Jesus Lord of all.
One kingdom of light within and without.
One universal life of God embracing –
Wisdom and Virtue, Holiness and Freedom – Peace.
One Godhead overall, One Church of Love in Unity.
Hallelujah! Glory to the Lord, Hallelujah! Glory to our Godhead of Love.

In the hedgerows and in God's garden I see the wild white rose which reveals the purity of Truth and Love, as of the Holy cross of Love, glorified as One Power to heal, and all shall be well. His amazing Grace is the hand of God; Love reaching down from the Divine centre touching us, linked with the created centre of his earth, an experience of Eternal Glory, light which penetrates all of cosmic origin. The Creator of all in Glory reigns supreme, for God of the All-Seeing Eye, knows all our thoughts and actions, and loving our neighbours?

("By grace you have been saved through Faith... it is the gift of God." Ephesians 2, v 8)

("The Lord is my light and my salvation: whom shall I fear?" Psalm 27, v 1)

("Yes!" I cry, thanks be to our Godhead of Love.)

Our God Reigns
One God who Loves us all as One

(July 13th 1983)

Jesus Lord in your amazing Love I see a cross of light beaming down from Heaven, in a dream or was it imagery? Much as Jacob saw a ladder, in a dream, so long ago. (With angels ascending and descending from the Throne of Grace.) A cross with arms outstretched embracing the whole world and Universe, having an intersection point of Love (the throne) central to Heaven and the Universe.

One cross of Love linked with the earth, yet of Heaven, for you Dear Lord and our Father God are One, One Heaven of rest, Peace, and Life to come. One cross of Love which has beamed down to us ten years of glorious revelations and ten years of visions. Spanning the space of time from Creation to this 'New Age' of Love renewed. Jesus your amazing Love has been manifested through your light supreme incarnated as One Holy Joy, One church of Love and Peace, into Eternity.

Dear God we thank you for your amazing Creation manifested; granted to us here in our bedroom one night revealing a large black circular ball spinning in space like some giant Catherine wheel (vision as from the floor to the absent ceiling) when crescent moons of light, stars, suns and mystical Heavenly bodies of light and colour were rapidly thrown off into space, One Creation of all matter in an age lost through the passage of time, yet lives on in universal Glory, Love manifested in all Creation, such Amazing Grace, such Love filled with his Love, all man made objects were obliterated; yet in some of the painted visions, I have shown some structure/furniture etc in order that the viewer is able to understand His Love more fully perhaps? Central here in Gods act of Love.

Jesus your oneness with the Father was again revealed on a moonlight night in our bedroom window of visions: of your Tau and Latin crosses granted in quick succession, of both ages, old and new.

A few days later from this window into Heaven you filled our room with a cosmic flow of Heavenly bodies of light, from the east, of colour, moons large and small, crescents, suns and stars of many shapes (as of Creation revealed) again revealing your Heavenly Creation as of the Godhead supreme. For to Love God and to Love our neighbours is to die for all (yet I continue to fail in total Love!) One church of Love in Unity, is God's will for all mankind.

Such amazing Love, amazing Truth and amazing Peace was granted to the prophets, saints, martyrs, and mystics of old. We read from the greatest book of Love of One universal God now makes all things new, One Divine Love able to relive, renew, resurrect and make all things new and all shall be well. (For Jesus died in order that all may be saved from hell, "Behold I make all things new." Revelations 21, v 5).

Meditation, Advent 1981 - December 1983

One Cross of Light and Love, One Golden Star

Dear God you sent us a golden star of light at Advent 1981 and again on Christmas night following a midnight Mass, the Lord's supper of Communion and after I read the Bible, early morning. One God who ever challenges us to prepare ourselves for a new golden age of One church of Love in Unity of Peace of three. One God of Love who ever challenges each of us to search for the Truth of "Who am I? Where am I going?" (A message to my soul received here on the pilgrims way each, over twelve months, as from the two hour trance July 18th 1976 to July 18th 1977).

On Good Friday, March 1982, our loving Father God through the soul once again confirmed the risen Christ, One church of Love. The time of this revelation of Love was at 2.22 p.m. during the latter part of a Good Friday three hour service conducted by a visiting priest from our coastal town of Eastbourne, Sussex.

After two hours of service in Holy Cross church, this preacher-teacher had built a mental picture of our dying Lord upon the cross.

Just prior to his announcing the penultimate hymn the crucifix (cross of death and new life) hanging on the wall by the pulpit, glowed with moving tongues of spiritual light from the edges of the three arms at the top (as of the one Tau and Latin cross, the Godhead).

No light was revealed from the created figure of Christ on the cross! For he is Eternally risen and such carved figures of our Lord are not of reality to me. There then flashed a narrow shaft of light shooting up to the roof and Heaven and at the same time a shaft of light from the base of the cross to the floor and the earth's centre of God's Creation? The priest then announced the hymn to follow and from the third line of the first verse we sang in unison:

"The cross shines forth in mystic glow."

Bishop Venantius Fortunatus (AD530-609) was the composer of this lovely hymn.

Once again I am reminded that "I have no knowledge except that which is revealed to me for carved images of our Lord, Mary and the Disciples are of no reality to me except they have first been granted by God through Divine visions to artist or the craftsman carving the image, for God rejected many images throughout the old testament we know. (December 1983).

Since this experience, the cross of risen Glory has been manifested in subsequent services when a preacher or teacher in a sermon touched on a spiritual revelation of Love. A bishop from South Africa preached here recently, below the crucifix, when this little wooden cross once again revealed the light at the top only, but not of the carved image of our Lord I noted neither was a ray of Light revealed going up nor coming down from the Cross, as on Good Friday 1982!

(And these signs shall follow them that believe, Mark 16, v 17).

From St Paul's Epistle to Hebrews Chapter 8, we have the promise of a New Covenant:

"...For this is the covenant I will make with the house of Israel after those days, says the Lord: I will put my laws into their mind and write them on their hearts: I will be their God, and they shall be my people."

(St Paul's Epistle to the Hebrews, Chapter 8)

"None of them shall teach his neighbour, and none his brother, saying 'Know the Lord' for all shall know Me, from the least to the greatest."

In these few lines I read the promise for the New Age, a theology for a 'Golden Age of Peace and Freedom'. Preparing and building a New Jerusalem preparatory to Jesus' second coming. "That they may all be One as I and the Father are One."

(Jesus' perennial call for Unity a new Revelatory and Revolutionary age: "Christ the Power of God and the wisdom of God?" 1 Corinthians 1, v 24).

And from 1 Peter 1, v 5. "Kept by the Power of God through faith unto salvation."

Here perhaps for the first time I have quoted from both St Peter and St Paul. The two Apostles from whom both Catholics and Anglicans claim apostolic succession? Yet the two are One in the Godhead of Love embracing all branches of the One True Vine.

A Garden Mouse

(30th July 1983)

It was but a few summers ago when I crossed our lawn close by the site of the mystic Latin and Tau cross revealed as One, to enter our kitchen home at the sound of the call of a sheep bell. The call to a meal, as of a call in the countryside, for centuries past, and the sheep bells on the Sussex downs which I often recall from the born-free experiences of my childhood days such as wandering in the Glory of God's Creation, the wild gorse on the downlands, and the Glory of the wild flowers around, all-glorious creation.

Our lawn here at this time was covered with white upturned faces of a thousand daisies, each having a golden eye reflecting the light of his Eternal Love. Quite suddenly I stopped to gaze at a wee mouse, for my right shoe almost covered it.

Sitting upright, it was delicately washing its face, fur and whiskers with its front paws, scooping the dew from the centre of a golden daisy bowl which she deftly continued to do: quite oblivious of my massive shoe, close by, yet observed I must have been, for our loving Godhead momentarily united us as One.

For in the simplicity and beauty of created life is revealed the greatest mystical beauty of all as St Francis of Assisi discovered, that Christ and the Father of Love is One in all. One life, One church of Love in Unity, One Eternal Godhead over all.

Robert Burns, a Scottish poet, was a true descendent of the Celtic age, I feel, who, like some Irish and Welsh and English people who speak only of the Godhead, of the One church, of the union of the Celtic Cross, of Creation, and the Jesus Latin cross, of Love, as One – One church of Love in Unity.

(R Burns)

'To a mouse on turning up her nest with the plough in November 1785.'

> Wee, sleekit, cow'rin', tim'rous beastie,
> O what a panic's in thy breastie…!
> I'm truly sorry man's dominion,
> Has broken Nature's social union,
> An' justifies that ill opinion
> Which makes thee startle
> At me, thy poor earth-born companion,
> An' fellow-mortal!

(John 17, v 23)

"I in them, and you in me, that they may be made perfect in One, and that the world may know that you have sent me and have Loved them as you have Loved me."

The harvest this year has been one of ripening fruits, vegetables and the blue grapes hanging on our stable wall. The vine, the symbol of our lord's great sacrifice this year, has grown so well perhaps to give us for the first time a gallon or two of choice wine later on perhaps? I recall a strange vision one night of a four-legged bird sitting on a branch of a bush or tree. It appeared to be as large as a pheasant having four shortish legs, two pointed forward, in the breast, and it was drinking from a coconut held above its head!

The flowers, trees and fruits reveal the hand of God so freely given and Peace walks in his garden each evening. When the sun goes down my soul rests in Love and Peace in He who Loves us all as One.

When we see Him we know Him to be Love, for He does not change in this changing world of man. For He is Love, and Love is Peace within.

One God One church of Love in Unity, the Godhead III.

"The word is... a light unto my path." Psalm 119, v 105.

> Wisdom exalteth her children and
> layeth hold of them that seek her.
> He that Loveth her Loveth life;
> and they that seek her early
> shall be filled with Joy. He that
> holdeth her fast shall inherit Glory:
> and wheresoever she entereth, the
> Lord will bless.

Ecclesiasticus 4, v 11-13.

"The Bible view is unique in its insistence on faith as the key that unlocks the gate of Heaven – not asceticism however severe, or thought however exalted, or deeds however sacrificial, or spiritual exercises however demanding. The Bible abounds with illustrations of this basic principle of faith, from Abraham to the writer of the Hebrews."

From Stuart Blanch, a former bishop in the Church of England, I believe.

"According to your faith be it unto you." Matthew 9, v 29.

John 8, v 31

"Turning to the Jews who had believed in him, Jesus said, 'If you dwell within the revelation I have brought, you are indeed my Disciples you shall know the Truth, and the Truth will set you free.'"

For such is the wonder and the Glory of God for throughout my life I have been searching for Reality. For with a lifetime of searching, and of trial and error, I have been seeking the true meaning of Love. This through God's Amazing Grace has been confirmed over and over again. The oneness of Christ and our Father God Creator is simply: 'Love Eternal'. Therefore all images of our Lord on the cross or of Mary, or of the many paintings I have seen are meaningless except that God has first granted the true image or revelation of Jesus to the mind, heart and soul to the Creator of the work of art, of the painter or sculptor I feel? (I apologise if I have written this earlier on.)

Advent 1983

Extract from our Diary of Discovery and Revelations

Over the past few days there have been great gales, and loss of life for a family of three near here were killed by a crashing tree, in this stormy weather and heavy rain. Yet yesterday being Advent Sunday, calm weather was restored to us once more. On our lawn this morning I observed three grey squirrels chasing each other amongst a variety of birds: a crow, starlings, blackbirds and a colourful jay, magpie, a woodpecker, pigeons, and quite a variety of smaller Song birds, one happy family of God. All were enJoying the plentiful supply of food to be found here on God's evergreen, ever provident garden table. A scene of Peace and harmony and Unity to come, I feel.

The three arms of an ageing apple tree in the centre of the garden are refusing, as yet, to surrender their summer Shroud. For there are still many green leaves to be seen. Suddenly a bright ray of piercing light from a sunbeam shines out of the grey clouds overhead, transforming this scene, for it strikes a pearl-like drop of dew on the lawn changing it into a diamond, ablaze with radiant light! What a contrast this was to the scene of last week of several days of glistening white blankets of sparkling hoarfrost of early mornings, to a new scene of great promise, new life to come.

Suddenly from the east there appeared three messengers of the Light, three seagulls gliding over the site of the unified Latin and Tau crosses. The Two crosses of Love † which appeared on God's evergreen lawn in the sixth month of 1975 and the Tau cross, T, in June 1980, God revealing that the two are unified as One, of Christ and our Father of Love, of Old Testament and New. One risen loving Godhead overall. I raised my eyes to the green hill in the east, beyond our valley, for there I could see a fresh green sheen of sprouting autumn sown grain, a green hill, not so very far away? New life has already begun on this second day of Advent! For the winter jasmine on the wall is full of yellow star-like flowers of promise for it grows just below our east bedroom window of visions from Heaven. (Though visions have been granted in our bedroom and in the Universe.)

Three grey and white collared wood pigeons now pecking on our lawn remind us of the One church of Love in Unity. God most surely reigns in his Heaven for I see Christ in all his radiant Glory walking upon the face of the earth and "all shall be well". And suddenly the birds rise up as One to alight in the trees and surrounding hedgerows as a white cat, a messenger of Peace of the Holy cross, appears. Nearby a silver birch now shining brightly in the sunlight heralds the coming of Christmas more clearly and more brightly than all the burning candles of Adventide for it is like a blazing light set upon a hill, God's open house, for all to see. In February, 1976 God sent four seagulls from the west, circling over the Latin cross site as One, then one flew over to the north, one to the south, one east and one west forming a Heavenly orthodox cross. In June 1981, three swans from the north circled once before flying in the form of a Latin cross, one to the north, one to the south and one west. The mysticism of God transcends all human thought pattern and leads us to meditate "And then you shall know the Truth and the Truth shall make you free." John 8, v 32.

For if we are born again of the spirit (spiritual renewal) we are indeed free to serve Christ and the Father of Truth in the oneness of his Love for all. For Christ said, "If thine eye be single (soul) thy whole body will be full of light." This light of the soul, is both Christ within mind, heart and soul and Christ without, for God has blessed us with ten years of all-glorious revelations and visions of the Unity and the oneness of Love.

In the years of Divine revelations I have become so aware of the symbol of three, of Jesus in dwelling in the mind, then in the heart then in the soul, the glorious Unity of the Godhead III. Of Creation and the revealed word of Love from the Bible.

Mary's Song of Love in Unity, 1983-1984

Sunday 24 July 1983

Last evening Beth read from her prayer book the Magnificat, Mary's Song of praise to God when visiting her cousin Elizabeth. After reading chapter 13 of St Paul's epistle to the Hebrews I then read Mary's Song from Luke. The scene was that of Elizabeth's home, three months prior to the birth of John the Baptist? Proclaimer of the Truth to come.

Having laid down the Bible (New King James Version) I once again experienced the light of the Holy Spirit as the natural light changed instantly to total darkness when a vision of two women in long grey dresses appeared in the east window, magnified by the soul.

In a flash the scene changed to one of Mary singing, sitting on a three-legged stool, holding a small Song book with both hands: Elizabeth was now revealed standing, yet facing Mary with elbows at her side, having her arms and hands facing upwards glorifying God. Suddenly Mary's face and head were revealed with great clarity and beauty, when the spirit of Truth, Love, and wisdom, caused her to burst forth into the Song of:

> My soul doth magnify the Lord,
> and my spirit has rejoiced in God my Saviour,
> for He has regarded the lowly state of His maid servant,
> for behold from henceforth all generations will call me blessed.
>
> For He who is mighty has done great things for me.
> And Holy is His name.
> And His mercy is on all those who fear Him,
> From generation to generation.
> He has shown strength with His arm;
> He has scattered the proud in the imagination of their hearts.
>
> He has put down the mighty from their thrones, and exalted the lowly.
> He has filled the hungry with good things, and the rich He hath sent empty away.
> He hath helped His servant Israel,
> In remembrance of His mercy.
> As He spoke to our Fathers,
> To Abraham and his seed forever.

(Luke 1, 46-55)

This was the third beautiful and realistic vision of Mary including that of the eve of Advent 1981 and of the three visions before Easter 1983 of Joseph, Mary and John the Evangelist as of Knock, Ireland near the middle of the last century? Only since this revelation of the 'Magnificat' have I truly understood the spirituality of Mary's prayer and Song to God. (Mary the chief or head of all saints I feel, from now on).

The earth's structure, the magnetic centre of the wind, waves, and tide, the sun and moon, affecting all life on earth. The mystery of the continuity of life?

Whenever I am at work in your garden or paddock Lord, I am never truly alone for in Jesus I see you dear Father of all. This Lovely summer of 1983 lingers on in the earth and in the Heavens when I see the wild 'V' formation of geese flying overhead from the east, each autumn and winter eventide, to their feeding grounds.

For the Father cares for all Creation, and Sons and daughters as One. Now I see two grey collared doves, side by side, sitting on our lawn, close by the site of the Latin and Tau crosses, unified as One.

Whilst rolling our lawn one day early in 1983, I paused close by the site of the crosses. On meditating on a recent act of murder in Northern Ireland, our Lord God spoke to my soul, for the fourth time, I believe? "The Protestants' minds are filled with the knowledge of the word, the Catholics minds with the knowledge of the saints." The date is recorded in our Diary which has not been typed since early 1983, True Unity alone will heal all branches of the 'One True Vine', for Love holds the key.

Truth and the Divine Power

(Extract November 11 1983)

Throughout my life there has been a growing awareness of the symbol of three: for Love is One Father – Creator, in the Unity of Son – Redeemer and loving spirit – Revealer. Through Jesus to the Father of all: One Father, Son and Holy spirit of the Godhead III.

Thus I feel that all adoration should be directed to these as One to our dear Lord, One God-Creator of all life and matter, for his beLoved Son Jesus who sacrificed his life in order that we may become One in Him and He in us. One Lord of all, One church in Unity of loving Holy Spirit. Remember, that we pray in Unity with the saints of both Old and New Testaments and those of the 2000 years of the Age of Christ and past, for Mary has been revealed as the Chief or Head of all Saints I recall.

The Holy Spirit in this Unity of three is the revealer of the true Love of Truth, One all glorious fellowship of three. One Creator, One Christ, One Spirit of Love combine to bring us to the knowledge of the One church in Unity of now into eternity, the Godhead III.

The oneness of Truth can only be found in these three of Truth of Creation, of the inspired, prophetic and revealed word of Christ and God of the Old Testament and New and of our Father God of the book of Love. Truth and Peace are one in the knowledge, and realisation of the presence of God both without and within, is One Light of Love. Renewal is to salvation, as Love is to Eternity, One church in Unity of Testaments Old and New.

His presence both underlies and transcends all mystical experiences of Truth, for he is both present within and without in the one sacrament of Love. for the word of God and sacrament of his body and blood are One in Unity, of Creation and of Christ and the Spirit revealed Word of the One church of Love, of Testaments Old and New.

For the loving Godhead reigns supreme of now and in Eternity. For Jesus said, "I am the way, the Truth and the life." The "I am" being One in the light of the loving Godhead within and without. Threefold Truth is only found through Love and searching: first of our wills, the work of the spirit of Love to the mind: Truth from mind to heart is of grace of the oneness of Love. Truth from heart to soul is also of grace, of true mysticism of Love of the sovereign Godhead supreme.

A tenant farm where three generations of my family lived. Attached was a Chapel erected in the late fourteenth century. From 1660-1698 in the cellars of our old home was founded in secrecy the Axminster Congregational Church. From then onward spread out the Branches of non-conformity (Bible-Lovers). Branches of the 'One True Vine' from the West.

After the Latin cross of hazelwood appeared at my feet mid-June 1975 an Angel of light of our Lord gripped my right arm twisting me around when my soul received this message "Write a diary of Discovery and Revelation." Thus I was led into our home to an armchair and with pain of the soul the Holy Spirit transported me back to the third floor of the bedroom where I was born 31st March 1916, Weycroft, Devon.

Over three whole days I was led to record sixty-five A4 sheets of a brief history of my life. Both by day and by night I experienced soul pain. I tried to read a few of the many lines of scribble but I failed to do so, and so, over the next three or four months I was led to write the whole of the writings through the grace of our Godhead of Love (sixty-five pages).

My family migrated to live and farm in East Sussex in March 1921.

That which I remember chiefly was an ancient well in our garden just off the Roman Fosse Way.

The Last Supper: As Revealed in the Godhead Forms

(vision granted on the ninth day of this Lovely month of June 1984)

Love and soul experience are One in the Unity of the light of the Godhead III. On this, the sixth visit of my soul to the supper chamber I looked down upon the long white supper table laid with our dear Lord of light. Standing central on the right, arms outstretched, praying and blessing the food, bread and wine, opposite was Peter standing? Hands together and six Disciples on either side of the table (when later I painted this, seemingly God led me to omit the one sitting on Our Lord's right, Judas I assumed?)

In stillness lies the mystery of the oneness of the light everlasting. For then our Lord and Peter sat down and the nearest disciple on my right broke off a portion of the loaf, passing it to the disciple opposite. The passing continued across the table creating an unbroken chain of triangles, as it were, linked as one throughout. However as the large loaf passed Jesus the passing accelerated and the last Disciple on the right passed the loaf very quickly to the one sitting opposite!

It was a Joyful scene, this supper of Love revealed to my soul, the Last Supper in fact as revealed.

The next day I was standing on the site of the crosses here meditating on the acceleration of the passing of the bread when God answered to my soul, "This is the manner in which all branches of the One True Vine will accelerate towards Unity by the end of the 2000 years of Christ," I thought just how wonderful God is to reveal and confirm his call to all – Unity by the end of 2000 years of Christ, after all Love is the golden key. One church of Love in Unity and eternity.

Praise be to our God of Love in Unity for this was the message of the unbroken chain of triangles, created by our Lord and the Disciples of Christ across the Last Supper table (thus God confirmed all the visions granted since 15th June 1973 with this Lovely message to my soul late January 1994 about the date of my dear mother's birthday.) "There is a light more bright than the midday sun, or the moon and stars by night. For it is the Light of Him who loves us all as one. One Holy church of Love."

(The Godhead III, Unity, embracing almost twenty-one years of Divine Revelations on this Holy Acre)

And from this time onwards we committed our Home garden and Holy cross acre to our all-glorious Godhead III for a future Healing centre of Love.

When God speaks to us it is of the three, for the still small voice of God first speaks to the lower region of the soul. The soul imparts this Truth in mystical reverse order to the heart. By grace the heart communicates this Truth to the mind. Thus we are conscious of doing "His will".

Mary I see as one of the great channels of grace leading us to Christ in the one family of God, on earth and of Heaven, of Love. Mary has been revealed as the chief of all saints with John the Baptist, holding the cross of Love, sitting upon her knee. Mary's Song is of the:

One Holy Church of Love in Unity: God Our Father

(Advent November 1984)

God has granted us the wisdom of knowledge that he is one in the inspired, prophetic and revealed word of Love, One Holy church in Unity of Creation, the Word and Sacrament of Love, of past, of now, and in eternity, One Godhead over all.

"Love is the way", "Love is the Truth", "Love is the life", "Love is the Glory". In all his ministry of three years as Man of God (God's Son) Christ gave us healing and his daily word for living. That wholeness which may be granted through a progressive seeking of Truth to the mind, Truth to the heart and Truth to the soul. God's will, and at the same time in our hearts having a desire for Truth and Justice.

In all I read, in all I see and in all I hear, touch, taste, and smell lies in the wonder of Love. One Holy church of Love revealed in living Glory. Father you are this Love, this Truth, this Glory; the One Eternal Light revealed in the Unity of three. In the wholeness of the gospel of Christ Jesus lies the oneness of Love linked with the prophecy of the saints, mystics, and prophets of the past ages.

Love alone has the Power to lead us into Truth, and Truth only is the food of Love and Unity of soul. Love alone has the Power to teach and heal, Love alone reveals the Power of God's Truth and Justice. Love only grants us Eternal life and Peace. One loving, living Godhead overall.

Jesus upon the cross, for us, no longer reveals the Power of sin to maim, kill and destroy, for the cross alone, points to save, for Christ is risen, healed and glorified, made One in him Father of all. Hence One Eternal light not of this world but born again of the all glorious Unity of Love, of God and man made one. The One universal Godhead reigns supreme as Love in III. (Carved images of Jesus on the cross made by man bear no relationship for Jesus had risen, and was glorified, almost 2000 years ago we know.)

I see a gay profusion of yellow star-like jasmine flowers hanging below our window of visions facing the East. With each sunrise at this Advent season I am awakened by the sweet notes of a robin red and a shy wren or two. Fine dew-like drops of rain are now falling upon God's garden: with each perfect drop of sparkling dew Jesus calls each one of us anew, "Come unto Me" and "be born again, renewed of Love" a second baptism of "Life renewed" that true hope and oneness of inner self of Love, the soul, in Unity.

One Holy church of Love in Unity, the Godhead III reigns in Glory Eternally.

11 November, 1984

Again on this eve, our good Lord granted us a trefoil vision of Mary and the Christ child on her lap. Anne with a child, and Elizabeth, and John the Baptist. Dear Jesus was wholly of light and was pointing his arms and legs forward. Suddenly he punched them out sideways: a sign that we should all be activated in doing His will! Now there are diversities of gifts, but the same Spirit, and there are differences of administrations, but the same Lord.

And there are diversities of operations, but it is the same God which worketh all in all.

(1 Corinthians 12, v 4-6)

The Oneness of Christ and our Father of Love

Today the sun rose on Bird-in-Eye Hill shooting rays of golden light upon our trees and valley green. The morning choir in the apple trees and hedgerows have already poured forth their grateful thanks in Songs to Him who Loves us all as one, announcing New Life, through Christ, and the Father of all, Unity.

Beauty is the earthly throne of God, when we listen to His quiet voice by the brook, in the reeds, and rushes sighing, in the water meadows spread over the valley below our home. Jesus walks there as He also does here in God's Garden of Love, now revealing signs of changing shades of many golden coloured garments just before the fall, foretelling a New Jerusalem to come, embracing all.

Let the busy world rush on, pass me by, for I care not for the pressures or institutions created by man, God created harmony that we should all be free and live in Peace. I can seldom see God in the ceaseless maze of wheels racing over the Pilgrims' Way which crosses our busy High Street (east to west) and that running north to south between London and the coast. I see no pony and trap there; how sad, for those of us who Love such things. The rooks, crows, pigeons and jackdaws, thrushes, blackbirds, seagulls and geese sometimes seen flying to and fro are to me the real messengers of freedom and Peace to come, like the flocks of pigeons, collared doves and other birds who fly into our garden daily, or, pass over God's mystical cross and garden of Love flying west to east, or east to west, and sometimes north to south, or in the reverse order.

That Peaceful haven which we so blindly seek cannot be found in the fruits of personal gain. Rather first examine our life within. Is it filled with Love, Joy, hope and knowledge of eternity in Mind, Heart and Soul? Eternal beauty can be found in all life created by Him, from the smallest daisy to a tree or a bird on the wing. Let the blind lead the blind, but you my friend should seek nature's paths where Jesus will lead you into the reality of light; of Love within.

That Unity of Love of God reigning both without and within. I first discovered God in the simplicity and beauty of Creation as a child. Today having been granted over one hundred visions God continues to reveal his will in the simplicity of visions granted from 1973. Amazing Love and Grace.

So little has changed in God's real garden since he created it for man to live in to enJoy? Not many species of plants, animal, bird and man have changed or have disappeared through the action of man or through climatic and physical changes over some millions of years. Yet God lives on in his Eternal Light and the Son continues to pour his invisible rays of radiant light upon us all, like rays of sunshine filtering through the tall trees of a woodland glade in early spring. Yet much of God's Creation is unchanging.

26th January, 1985

After Bible reading evening, when it was dark, God revealed a dark human head form. Then a crucifix appeared central when golden rays of light shot out from the edge of our Lord's body on the cross, arms and head and legs, and from the edges of the cross.

This was granted to my soul six nights before Archbishop Desmond Tutu was proclaimed Bishop of Johannesburg, South Africa.

(After I cried out, "Get thee behind me Satan," and crossing myself, but the Revelation was of our loving Godhead, and it continued for a time.)

On quite a number of previous occasions when a Bishop, Canons, Priests, Curates, Deacons and Lay Readers have expounded the word of God this little cross has blazed forth, sometimes tongues, sometimes glowing spiritual light on the top edges only. God continues to call through revelation, his whole church, through Love and light, to renewal. Through repentance comes healing; the true inner self healed through the spirit and the inspired revealed word. The prophetic teaching of the old testament and the revealed word (church) of the new. The oneness of the Godhead of Love II. (Later on at night, I was in the spirit in Holy Cross looking up to the east window – Jesus forgiving Mary Magdelen. Then the spirit led me back to the nave to look up to the pulpit to see a large open Bible of the early church, the call to Anglicans to return to the wholeness of the Bible, prime source of worship and grace.

Only through perseverance, seeking, looking, watching, loving and doing God's will, listening, and in silence can we be "born again of the spirit".

Jesus' indwelling in the mind, heart and soul can lead to the all-glorious reality and revelation of the "One church of the loving Godhead" for our God reigns throughout the earth and Universe, the awareness of the totality of Creation through Love.

From the Old Testament we have, "the Lord answered me and said write the vision and make it plain upon tables, that he may run that readeth it. For the vision is yet for an appointed time, but at the end it shall speak and not lie; because it will surely come, it will not tarry."

Habbakuk 2, 2-3.

(Thanks be to our God of Love.)

(I believe that I have recorded twenty-one occasions when the Latin cross has glowed, but only at the top of the arms. The Godhead call for all branches of the 'One True Vine' to return to the Bible as the prime source of grace. All teachers and preachers take note for the cross has for almost 2000 years now revealed the Godhead call, to work and pray for the Unity of Love. In the two hour trance July 18th 1976 God advanced my soul to the end of 2000 years of Christ age the dawn of true Unity of Love. The Godhead III (third millennium). Lead on victorious Emmanuel.

Light of the Universal Church of Love

(27th Jan 1985)

This Sunday evening (28th January 1985) during EvenSong in Holy Cross Church the little crucifix on the wall of the pulpit once again shone forth in mystic glow. The priest was addressing us on the growing need for prayer and Bible study. Suddenly a small circle of spiritual light appeared on the wall to the right of the cross (crucifix). It faded and reappeared again, then, filling the top three arms of the cross with moving tongues of light, a ray of light shot downwards to the floor and the earth's centre beneath?

(On a Good Friday in the past this first happened when a narrow ray of spiritual light shot Heavenwards and to the church floor and earth centre.)

As the preacher-teacher continued a human form or outline of bright spiritual light blotted out the artificial light falling upon the wall behind the priest; then, as he ended his address this spiritual form faded. Never was the carved figure of Christ revealed! God continues to call his church to repentance, renewal and revelation. (The Divine will is hidden in every experience and in the Divine will, we find the Divine order.) H.T. Hamblin (we thank you). The Godhead III.

("We are looking forward to a new Heaven and new earth." 2 Peter 3, v 13)

(For Jesus said, "Come follow me.")

Remembrance Day - November 11th 1 a.m. 1984

Advent 1984 - The King of Glory - The One early Church of Love

Having read the Bible (psalm 68) I then laid it down to rest, King David's psalm of national triumph of Love, following a short prayer I was filled with his Love, and then granted a vision in the east window of visions into Heaven. There three women in grey appeared seated in the form of a trefoil leaf. The timelessness of Love revealed, three mothers and children three.

In the centre was a child of some twelve to eighteen months standing on Anne's lap (I sensed) Mary's Mother? To her right was Elizabeth with John the Baptist, a child standing, perhaps of the same age looking at Jesus, to the left, there was revealed Mary, of light grey, clearly defined, with the Christ-child Jesus (three-six months of age? wholly of light unclothed) sitting upon her lap looking forward with hands and feet pointing forward.

Suddenly, Jesus full of light, kicked out both his legs sideways and also thrust out his clenched hands and arms with some force sideways in uniSon. Oh what Joy filled my mind, heart and soul to both see and know of his Eternal loving presence within, this child of Love of some three to six months of age, God revealing his Love for all, the young, and mothers too, in this momentous year of 1984.

On Sunday, November 18th, dear Jesus was again revealed. But now some thirty three years or so later, dying upon his Father's cross. Jesus dying upon Friday's tree was revealed in miniature on a cross so very far away for it appeared to be only twelve inches high (to my soul?) yet to us for the first time, (before his resurrection) his body radiated light! For his Eternal light (as of the soul) was ever thus, united in God, him the Father of Love, and he in us, One Godhead over all, the One Eternal church of light and Love Eternal.

One loving Godhead reigns supreme.

For did he not also say, "A thousand years is but a day." The timelessness of visions lasting, sometimes a few seconds? sometimes a minute or two? and sometimes perhaps five or more minutes? I cannot say. And the two hour experience of the trance (ref: clock at my bedside), God only can reveal past experiences of Truth in eternity.

For Jesus said, "A little while and you will not see me," and again "a little while and you will see me" (his time is meaningless in eternity).

(John 16, v 16-17)

Jesus Lover of my Soul: Our God Reigns

(Advent 14th December 1984 to 3rd February 1985)

At midnight filled with his Love, our Lord God granted us a vision of Mary presenting the Christ child Jesus, full of light to Simeon at the Temple door. Dressed in a long dark robe he stood on the right side at the Temple door. Mary, less than three feet away to the left held the Christ-child of light with both feet and hands pointing forward, sitting on her palms with her forearms stretched forth. Jesus (unclothed) full of light looked forward as if to be received by Simeon at the Temple door?

Away to the left was revealed a dim grey human form, of a figure in a long robe, holding a staff. Joseph, I thought, filled with humility and awe, at the wonder of Mary's virgin-birth, child of light, Jesus the saviour of the world to come the child of God who one day, called to us both, Beth and me, "Come follow me" (Godhead III).

How truly wonderful and mystical is our Lord God of Eternal light. Granting as he so often has done all glorious revelations of the king of Glory, some time before the renewal of great historical events now about to be renewed this Christmas, the virgin-birth of Truth and Eternal light of Love. Hallelujah, the king of Glory reigns supreme.

When Christmas comes again this year I intend to hang our largest and brightest three electric lanterns high up on the branches of a silver birch tree in God's garden of revealed Eternal Love, through the crosses of the Old Testament and the New. To shine out, to the north, east and west, and southwards, these bright lights will blaze out over God's island garden-home, One garden and fields of our valley green, to the homes beyond. Proclaiming his birth, resurrection, and Eternal light and all glorious life. Lights of the all glorious Godhead of Love, made hope a reality here, over some eleven all glorious years now, granted to us through Love.

"You are my friends if you do what I command" John 15, v 14. (The Vine and its Branches). Isaiah the great prophet of old in 740 BC declared a message for the salvation of the people of Ireland and of the United Kingdom. I feel, and also for all: Nations, if we love Jesus and our Father God as One: The Godhead III.

"Listen O isles unto me and hearken ye people from afar; the Lord both called me from the womb from the bowels of my mother hath he made mention of my name. And he hath made my mouth like a sharp sword; on the shadow of his hand hath he hid me, and made me a polished shaft in his quiver hath he hid me and said unto me, 'Thou art my servant.'" Isaiah 49, v 1-3.

(Whenever I read this I feel it confirms God's call to my soul from birth. Again, Amazing Grace).

Meditations on the Healing of Divisions. PEP (Mrs)

Experience 1

Standing by the laurel tree in our garden in Uckfield, Sussex, and close by the patio terrace, I was, one afternoon, startled by a beautiful bluish-green dragonfly which flew into my face knocking my cheekbone hard. This made me think of Ringmer, a village about six miles away. I had been there to a flower and craft festival the day before and had seen on their brochure that there would be Mime and Dance that evening at Ringmer village hall called Dragons and Dumplings. The Mime and Dance were to be introduced by a Mr Philip Curtis. His name reminded me of our former family doctor whose name was Bryce-Curtis. He served our family for over thirty-five years. As I was meditating I realised that God was calling me to got out to Ringmer that evening. I carried with me some of my healing writings to give to the St Mary's Church Youth Group who were taking part and also one for Mr Curtis. They welcomed me when I arrived, but I was not allowed to watch as the Mime and Dance were only for participants and not spectators. However I didn't feel it was a wasted journey as, before departing, I met a Brownie Guider and a Brownie Guide with her mother who led me to the Brownie Guide Pack Meeting at an adjoining room in the village hall. Afterwards I came across a St John's Ambulance Group Meeting in a room at the far end of the Hall. First Aid and Home Nursing were being taught the young. Both meetings were very pleased to receive some healing writings.

Experience 2

Walking past the gateway to Firle churchyard in Sussex after attending an exhibition in the village hall of old photographs and regalia of past village life in Firle, my husband and I noted a white swan sitting motionless on a grave. It seemed strangely still, and then my husband remarked, "I wonder if it is sitting on my cousin Heber's grave?" I answered, "I hadn't realised that your cousin had been buried in this churchyard." I remember him telling me of his cousin's tragic death, a suicide, at the farm in Firle where his family moved to in the 1930s. We decided that we would come back the following week to seek the grave, as we didn't have time then. The following week we found the grave. It was quite near to the church doorway, and had a very nice headstone. We saw that Heber's wife Elsie was also buried there. We met the vicar's wife who was going into the church and asked her why there were so many swans sitting in the churchyard. We could see several settled and nestling on the graves. She told us that they came from the lake at Firle Place and that they seemed to find the churchyard a very warm and sheltered place to settle, because of the high hedges.

Some weeks later I was meditating on this experience and thought of Lindfield, a pretty village in West Sussex well known for its swans on the village pond. I then thought of Mr Linfield who tended the graves at Uckfield Parish Church of the Holy Cross. I had often spoken with him in the churchyard, and now felt that I ought to visit him and his wife at home in Streatfield Road, Rocks Park, Uckfield. They were very pleased to see me, and realised I had been led to them. Mr Lindfield had to leave for a funeral as he works for the local undertakers, but before leaving he kindly gave me a bag of windfall apples from the boot of his car. I was so grateful as we hadn't any apples.

Experience 3

A fortnight before Christmas and near to our Ruby Wedding, my husband and I felt we would like to visit the old Strict Baptist Chapel called Jirch at Haywards Heath where we were married forty years earlier. We arrived on Sunday morning for the weekly service, and found everything much as we remembered it to be. Nothing seemed to have changed. An elderly minister from Rye was preaching. We also spoke with the organist who actually recognised me after all those years. Her father had taught my brother and I in the Sunday School. She introduced us to her husband who was the Deacon. We then went to sit in the old family pew where I had sat with my parents for so many years of my youth. I remember mother pushing the pram there with my younger sister in it and my brother sitting beside me with my father in the pew. We also saw father's old Bible still there with his name on it. This all brought tears to my eyes as time seemed to have stood still. Then I noticed that I had put my gLoves beside the Bible and on top of the gLoves I saw a little floret of yellow winter jasmine. I said to my husband, "Look, I must have carried that all the way from home. Fancy it clinging to my glove like that. I must have brought some flowers into the house before leaving and one must have fallen on to my glove sticking to it all the way." The winter jasmine bush grows up our house wall close to our French windows in the kitchen. I said, "I shall leave it in the pew here as an omen for good. Don't you remember you once had a vision of three yellow lemons on a branch over the Bibles in our bedroom, and it was all in colour?" My husband said, "Yes, I remember it."

Some weeks after Christmas I was meditating on the yellow floret clinging to my glove. This led me to want to get in touch with Mrs Thomson-Glover. We had met her every year for three or four years at the summer meetings of the Focolare Movement at Hull University. This ecumenical movement of the Catholic Church is centred on the Unity of Christians and especially on Jesus Christ's message, Where two or three are gathered together in my Name, there I am in the midst of them." Mrs Thomson-Glover was a very kind and charming person with whom we quickly made friends. She told us that she also lived in Sussex but in the western part. We noticed that she was blind in one eye, which was rather disfiguring. We found her to be such a loving and humble person that we couldn't feel shy or uncomfortable talking to her as she quickly put us at ease. I have now written to tell her how I was led to get in touch with her at her home in West Chiltington. She had so kindly sent us postcards when away on holidays abroad. I met her recently with my daughter and grandchildren at a holiday meeting at Bangor in Wales in the summer.

Experience 4

In February this year I saw a beautiful rainbow, the base of which was on the Pilgrim's Way footpath in Framfield. The footpath passes through Hempstead Farm near Sandy Lane. The rainbow made a very high arc over the Hempstead Fields, Hempstead Lane and Brown's Lane. I remembered that this happened on my son-in-law's birthday. He is a coloured Mauritian and I told him about the rainbow when he returned from work. I said it could have some symbolic significance for him and for coloured people. Some weeks later I was meditating about the rainbow, and realised my husband was at that very same time at Chubb's Nurseries at Cooksbridge buying a Greengage tree and a Victoria Plum tree for our garden. Then I remembered I had taught two young Catholic boys whose names were Leighton and

Stuart Chubb in the Brownsea Cub-Scout Pack which is part of the Holy Cross Church Scout Group in Uckfield. Recently, while joining in prayers for Ireland and St Philip's Roman Catholic Church in New Town, Uckfield, I spoke to Sister Lucy and Mrs Stayne about the rainbow. Sister Lucy knew the Chubb boys very well and told me that they still attend the church and were progressing very well in the education, although when they were younger they had suffered through their parents' broken marriage.

My husband and I wish to share these experiences with you and your friends and families.

Further Meditations on the Healing of Divisions

Experience 5

Sitting by the fire one spring evening, I was startled by some sparks and cinders falling from the fire on to the black rug where I was sitting. My husband and I hastened to pick them up to avoid the carpet underneath from being burnt into a hole. Some time later I could still smell burning and thought that we had failed to retrieve all the cinders from the rug. After a while, my husband asked if I had anything cooking on the stove in the kitchen and after a pause, I suddenly remembered I had put some ravioli on the stove to cook, some time before. I rushed into the kitchen to find it full of smoke and the small pyramid saucepan blackened with heat. I managed to take off the lid and out floated ash.

Meditating on this occurrence afterwards, my thoughts flew to Italy and the Focolare Movement, at the same time remembering the Byrnes family, whom we had met at one of their meetings in Hull some years previously. We had not been in touch with them for some years. Mr Byrnes, I remembered, was a warehouseman in Cleveland and he and his wife were head of our house group. These thoughts made me very soon get in touch with the family. They soon replied, saying how pleased they were to hear from us again and they told us that they were praying for us and that they believed that the Holy Spirit was in our midst.

Experience 6

A few weeks later my husband and I were invited to tea at Wellingham Lane, Ringmer. Whilst we were having tea in the lounge, a bird came to the window near to where my husband and his brother were sitting. It began to tap the glass with its beak and continued to do so for some time. My husband's brother noticed that it was a pied wagtail. This bird was getting to be quite a nuisance as it wouldn't go away, but persisted in tapping the glass with its beak and claws. The curtain was eventually pulled across to distract the wagtail. However, after a while, it came to the other window in the room where I and my husband's sister were sitting and continued the process once more with its beak and claws, until dusk when we were leaving the house for home.

Afterwards, meditating on this happening, my husband and I were led in our thoughts to Hannover, Germany where our son lives. When staying with him, he took us to the town of Hamelin, now far away, where on Sundays, during the summer months, the citizens of the town, enact the play the Pied Piper of Hamelin, which is well known for its legend. My husband, continuing to meditate on this, was immediately led to think of his cousin Ida, who lives also in Ringmer. She is a teacher and taught for many years at the British Forces School in Hamelin, and made many German friends. She now is headmistress of the Barcombe Village School.

"They shall speak of the Glory of they kingdom and talk of thy Power, to make known to the Sons of men His mighty acts."

Psalm 145, v 11-12.

From Paul's Epistle to the Romans 8, 28-30, we have a prediction of the calling and the fruits of the Godhead of Love.

> And we know that all things work together for good for those who Love God, to those who are called according to his

purpose. For whom he foreknew, he also predestined to be conformed to the image of his Son, that he might be the first born among many brethren. Moreover whom he predestined these he also called; whom he called, these he also justified and whom he justified these he also glorified.

For such is the wonder and the Glory of the Godhead III granted through over one hundred and sixty visions following Bible reading at night (from both the Old and New Testaments) and morning, for over twelve years now. By day, over three hundred and twenty revelations of God's Creation confirming the Truth of visions granted through Love. Very frequent bird activities above the site of the two crosses and over our small stable, which God revealed one night "the stable is to be called the Chapel of Christ and our Father of Love" (The Godhead III of healing). For Jesus said, "I am the way, the Truth and the life. No man cometh unto the Father but by me." John 14, v 6. For the revelations granted here are of the Unity and oneness of the Godhead III of the third millennium (foreknowledge of the Godhead III in Glory).

Eternal Love

(Good Friday and Saturday nights 7th April 1985)
Good Friday Night

Jesus Divine, your One great sacrifice for all mankind was again confirmed last night: thank you dear Lord. For God revealed you on this occasion from the side, nailed to Friday's tree, central at Calvary. Below this cross in the turf was revealed a human head form, having the One All-Seeing Eye of God: as granted on a few occasions in our window of visions for our God of Love who both sees and knows all; is ever near.

Suddenly at the back of the cross stood a lonely woman. Dear Mary our Lord's mother sorrowing for her Son. Then our great God of mystery (unseen by my soul) elevated Mary to the level of our Lord's head central to the cross. In a flash this vision vanished into the darkness of night. Then two women stood side by side. One was

Mary full of grief, and the other no doubt Mary Magdelen who also loved our Lord, foretelling his sacrifice for all upon the cross and later in the tomb.

Easter Saturday Night

During the night our Lord awakened me with three taps on our headboard of trefoil form. Filled with his Love my soul was once again granted a vision of Jesus dying upon the cross from a side view. To the left a few metres away, was a figure looking up, to Jesus, who was perhaps speaking? Was this figure Mary, or was it John to whom our Lord of Love committed His Mother for care? I do not know but Jesus' Love was instantly revealed for two rays of spiritual soul light central to that from our lord's soul one to the head, and one to the heart of this lonely figure. Thus for the second time our Lord God of Love has revealed his grace through Love confirming:

(1) Truth to the mind
(2) Truth to the heart, the harbour of the soul
(3) The Unity of the soul made one with the Godhead.

"He in me" and "I in him" one Love Eternal, overall. Throughout this experience in the turf at the foot of the cross was again revealed the head form and All-Seeing Eye of our glorious Father Godhead. Slowly fading into darkness, this vision appeared once more and then disappeared in a flash.

"He showed himself alive by many infallible proofs." Acts I 3, v7.

"He himself bore our sins in his own body on the tree that we, having died to sins, might live for righteousness" "by whose stripes you were healed." I Peter 2, v 24.

The One Godhead of Love, Truth and Eternity

(30th July 1985)

In the midst of thinking God is in the midst of loving is God. In the midst of Love we call to God and he hears us in the midst of meditation our Godhead embraces us, One God, One church of Love in Unity of three.

Now sings my soul to thee dear Lord, in thankfulness of twelve years of glorious visions, magnified of the soul, "walk in the way, walk in the Truth, walk in the light of Love. Walk, walk, walk in the Love of our Lord. Walk, walk in the Godhead of Love, holding fast to his staff of light".

Jesus Christ keeper and Lover of my soul, you sent us a messenger of light on a November day a few years ago when I was at work in your vegetable garden. The sudden appearance of a Red Admiral butterfly revealed your ever loving presence. Close to the site of the Latin and Tau cross unified as One. Walk, walk, in the freedom of Love in Unity.

Encircling my legs, our friend caused me to stop and stare when it alighted on a fallen green apple, symbolising the fruits of the earth. Slowly it opened its glorious wings to reveal the Eternal message of Truth, of Christ's redeeming Love, sacrifice and resurrection, (of the crimSon circle of Love) fruit of the spirit, the One Godhead of Love reigning Eternally, the kingdom within, and the wing tip lights of Heaven!

Suddenly our friend rose up to fly towards its winter habitat, carving before my eyes this message "Freedom" in the morning air. The one gift of Love "Peace" through the Unity, for with the human eye God grants us the wisdom of Truth. For with the crimson circle set in two dark brown wings of beauty revealed, "new life" beyond this earthly world of sin.

And all shall be free, and all shall be free, and all manner of things shall be free, as with all of God's Creation.

New life in Christ and he in us, through repentance, through renewal: One life, One sacrifice of Love, One kingdom of light, born again, risen from the tomb I see, for on each wing tip was revealed white splashes of cosmic lights. The universal Godhead reigns supreme in Unity and Love.

With each glorious vision revelation I am always made aware of the fact that I have no knowledge except that which is revealed to myself.

(John 17, v 10. Jesus prayer of Love to the Father – "And all mine are yours and yours are mine and I am glorified in them").

Thus all Divine revelations are foretold in the Glory of the Holy Bible.

"For he who has seen me has also seen the Father."

"The word for today is pray." John 16, v 14. "The Holy Spirit shall glorify me for he shall receive of mine, and show it unto you."
And from a meditation, 'God and the soul' by Canon D.W. Grundy, I discovered one of the greatest Christian thinkers. St Augustine spoke for us all when he wrote, "My desire to know God and the soul nothing else? Nothing at all." (Thanks be to God I cry! For no greater Truth can be revealed upon earth to all mankind!)

Jesus, Lover of my Soul

(Maundy Thursday Eve 27th March 1986)

This evening by our fireside I read from a booklet just one verse from the Bible. John 14 v 21 (from a televised service by Cliff Richard) "He who has thy commandments and keeps them it is he who Loves Me. And he who Loves Me will be Loved by my Father and I will Love him and manifest myself to him."

The hour was 10.30 p.m. and Beth and our son C (home for Easter holiday from West Germany) had just retired for the night. I fell asleep and was suddenly awakened at 11 p.m.! The six lights in our lounge were shining brightly, to my amazement a human figure (Jesus) full of light stood central holding the staff of light in his right hand. For a brief time I gazed in awe and then I arose from my armchair, scarcely believing this a reality, not of the human mind or heart but of the soul. The revealed word of God, our dear Lord Christ, my Saviour present on this Holy Acre, God's garden home.

The vision vanished as I moved one step towards the door to go upstairs to meditate on grace and to sleep in Peace. On the stairs which I climbed slowly, I meditated. Was this really Jesus or was this human form of light perhaps a disciple?

In the bedroom I spoke to Beth of the experience and she replied, "If Jesus was holding the staff it was a call to the mission field!" For God had already granted a vision of His Resurrection holding his staff of light!

And so I decided perhaps I should take photocopies of the painted visions to Hannover in West Germany in May this year, through soul travel. This manifestation was as that granted to us at night Jan 9th 1983 when Jesus glorified by our Father God burst through the great light that shone over the tomb in Gethsemane. Holding fast to the staff of light (Psalm 23). (Then I had just read Paul's Epistle to the Romans C12 before sleeping.)

Now in our bedroom I read a chapter from my Bible and after praying fell asleep. Soon after the Lord granted a pale grey trefoil vision in our window of light. Jesus as a young child was revealed standing in the central trefoil. Only Mary's torso was now revealed, without a head or the lower portion of her legs! Thus Jesus lying back on Mary's bust and whose head was most clearly revealed. Jesus of the loving Godhead III. The clover trefoil leaflets were of pale green.

The Universal Godhead of Love

(9th June 1986)

Beth and I returned rested on the 6th of June from our holiday in West Germany following our stay with our son in Hannover.

During the night of June 9th the Lord awakened me to experience the beautiful white star of King David. On praying and giving God thanks, this bright white star vanished. This light, His light, increased throughout the east window where our Lord then appeared so clear and human-like central, nailed to the cross of Calvary in a heart form of light. To his right in a grey head-form was revealed the All-Seeing Eye of God!

This soul vision faded rapidly when I prayed, thanking our God of Love. During the early hours of the morning the spirit awakened me again, revealing the east window full of light having three vertical rows of four figures in long robes of light grey. Central was revealed in a head form, the All-Seeing Eye of God as before.

To the lower left also was revealed the clear head of the lion of Judah (the Twelve Tribes of Israel) I then understood. Later I meditated on his experience in relation to the rebirth of the One church of the Godhead III. God has a purpose and message with all true visions granted through Love. My human interpretation of any experience may end and it will be open to question, for the Lord called me to challenge the institutional Churches and not to be the interpreter of visions as well! Pray to our Lord of Love who Loves us all as one, please.

Not until the whole of the diary of Discovery and Revelation has been completed, typed, edited etc., can the wholeness of the revelations be assessed or understood, I feel. For the incidences of bird-flight phenomena have been far more numerous than the visions. A full publication of the whole, I feel, must be achieved in my life time on earth. From my recollection there have been granted at least one hundred and fifty beautiful visions since the trance on July 19th 1976.

Meanwhile the Lord has called me to paint the visions. This may take some years. Then photographs of these could be published for I was primarily concerned with the Truth and Justice, from childhood days.

The call to my soul I first recall was on my grandparents' farm at 'Kinders', Devon, "Stand up for Truth and Justice." To the soul which I understand more fully today after forty-seven years of great mental activity in sending out thousands of records of the visions and revelations world wide. Mahatma Gandhi believed in spiritual freedom for all people, for he was called of God. All thanks be to our Godhead in Glory.

On Thursday evening of 21 March 1986, at 10.30 p.m., I was reading in our lounge John 14 v 21, and I fell asleep for half an hour. At 11 p.m., the eleventh hour, I was awakened to see both with my eyes and soul, Jesus wholly of light holding His staff of light for He stood looking at me in my armchair. His staff, the call to a prophet to declare the Divine (6) Revelations to all people as called of God in the two hour trance. July 18th 1976.

At the age of four, I was staying for four weeks at my grandparents' house, 'Kinders Farm', Axminster, Devon. It was apple-picking time and I can still recall those happy days. Each eve, sitting at a round supper table with Grandpa and Grandma, whom I loved dearly. For there, one day, or night, God spoke to my soul, "Stand up for Truth and Justice." Every night Grandpa read a chapter from the Bible as I sat opposite him, before Grandma's supper commenced.

From our marriage, December 1948, Beth and I regularly attended the Anglican and Strict Baptist Services on Sundays. A few years later we experienced fellowship with the Focolare R.C. Evangelical Movement through their monthly literature of Bible fellowship, and occasional church meetings in fellowship.

And so at the end of twenty-one years, after a loving fellowship with all three, I received three messages to my soul, yet from the local Baptist services of meditation, three message to my soul:

1. "The Lord hath need of thee."
2. "I have no knowledge except that revealed to me."
3. "My grace is sufficient for thee."

For the Lord's Prayer has been a prayer calling all to Unity for nearly 2000 years now. All the Divine experiences granted we feel are but a continuation of those of St Julian of Norwich 1373, for She loved her Bible, no doubt.

From the Bible – Introduction to the Prophets

The nature of prophecy:

1. The prophet in Israel is a mouthpiece; he has no doubt that the "Word of God" has come to him, and whatever method he uses to reveal it, he is a man to whom the Holiness and the will of God have been revealed.

2. He contemplates present and future through the Eyes of God, and is a man sent to remind the Nation of its duty to God and to bring them back to obedience and Love.

(Yes God has confirmed that "True Love" is reborn through loving the Bible and working and praying for Unity of all branches of the 'One True Vine', loving our neighbours.)

1. 10.2.87

Evening, awake, after reading Acts 32 and praying for the Beirut captives, including Terry Waite, the All-seeing Eye of God was granted in our east bedroom window of visions. The eye then grew into the form of a white orthodox cross with eight rounded curved corners. The prophetic cross of the Godhead III Unity? Then out of the centre shot a seven point golden star down over the three Bibles at our bedside. (Just one of God's thirteen Revelations calling attention to all branches of the 'One True Vine' (foretold by Jesus) to return to the Bible as the prime source of Grace, Healing of Divisions, and worship by the end of 2000 years of Christ. (I have been led to paint these two blessed Divine Revelations from our loving Godhead III, the experiences to all Nations. Thanks be to God. Thy will be done, in Communion).

2. It is with respect to this second verse that I recall later I was granted at least two Revelations of the All-seeing Eye of God, one at 6.45 a.m. 18.3.87, when God granted to my soul a vision of a light circle in the Universe, with the All-seeing Eye of God central in a pale blue sky full of stars. Then out of each corner of the Eye there grew out sideways the two long hands and arms of God. Slowly the hands turned facing each other and came together in prayer. As the fingers touched this vision to my soul ceased. Amazing Grace.

14th October 1987

Trees for me and perhaps many are linked with Eternal value for their life span may range from one hundred years to one thousand years plus or two thousand, as with the yew. There is a sense of agelessness from the Celtic age right through 2000 years of Christ. I believe the Druids valued them in their worship for I have read that the birch, willow, rowan, hazel, apple, ash, alder and the oak were eight trees of great significance to them in the pre-Christ generations. Just as I had written these few lines, the spirit led me to look up to the sky over the site of the crosses where I could see a heron flying overhead. It then flew slowly toward the high hedgerow and settled for a time in a large female holly tree close by.

9th May 1988

We were staying for a holiday in our son's flat in Hannover. Seven days after our arrival at night, after Bible reading, I was awakened from my sleep as a pair of blue eyes looked into my eyes. Next day, I gathered that my roots were of Anglo-Saxon origin? (North Germany?)

1st June 1988

After we had returned home to England, at Sunnybrooke Farm, at night, I had a dream of passing by an open door of our stable, where I noted bales of straw or hay piled up on the floor and on the top was a ginger cat with mewing kittens. I then walked to the doorway on the north side of our stable. There on the top of the bales was crouched a huge male lion ready to spring. It looked me in the eyes then lowering its head between it paws, it appeared to go to sleep!

14th June 1988

After Bible reading, awake, on the ceiling of our bedroom, God granted a vision of a white gosling or wild goose and young goslings. This was replaced with a vision of a mallard duck and ducklings. Then it changed to a group of smaller ducks or teal.

21st June 1988

Today a 'painted lady' butterfly appeared on our terrace in sunshine and settled on an open flower.

A white dove of Peace flew into our circular garden plot of flowers and then settled close to a patch of wild poppies which had grown very tall, with flowers twice their normal size. This was the other side of our drive, and it was, I felt, calling my attention to see this patch of poppies.

So I crossed the roadway where, to my amazement, I noted they had grown into the form of a cross. In fact a Latin and a Tau cross and also an Orthodox cross woven together as one. Amazing Grace.

I then walked up the Celtic bank to stand on the site of the three grass crosses from where the three wild poppy crosses to the east were clearly visible. The three grass crosses are over the site of our old well filled with soil. A Holy Well, of generations past?

3rd September 1988

In the afternoon I painted a white sphere of light which grew out of a glorious rainbow across a strip of soft white cloud. Then the west portion of the white sphere turned to gold. This was directly above the local St Philip's Catholic Church on the Eastbourne Road. We visit this church periodically on Saturdays to pray for Healing in Ireland.

A vision granted at night when our Lord God had revealed a military group of horsemen in a ceremonial parade. Central was a Victorian nursing chair on horseback. Close by was the mother on horseback, three generations of a Victorian family I felt?

10th March 1989

After reading I Samuel, v 48-49, to my soul at night Our Lord revealed a high square peg-board covered with perhaps over one hundred tools hanging from a mass of hooks. A short time later to my soul the Lord revealed in colour a young girl with dark auburn hair wearing a bright dress of green. Symbols of freedom to some in Ireland one day? I felt.

20th March 1989, Palm Sunday

After lunch I fell asleep, when in a visionary dream the Princess Margaret approached our stable in order to tie up her horse. Then I awoke. Later on God spoke to my soul, "The stable is to be called the chapel of Christ and our Father of Love", the One Church in Unity, of Healing to come, I sensed?

In the evening before going to sleep, I read the last chapter of Genesis, when later, our Lord God revealed the All-Seeing Eye when a white Greek cross grew out of it.

23rd March 1989

A soul experience of a crashed electric train across the fields one day close by? Then a square tablecloth was laid by two young men on the grass south of our terrace. Then four of us sat down to a meal.

24th March 1989

Vision when awake of a white tablecloth with a cake central and other food. A small girl and boy were sitting close to the cloth. A white cat and a hen were close by and also one or two other small animals. I had read Leviticus chapters 18 and 19 just before. At 9.30 a.m. the next day, there was a knock on our door but no one was there at the door I noted! The Devil once again, no doubt, troubling me!

25th March 1989

Easter Saturday three wild geese from the east flew over the three cross site. Later, six geese from east-west came over.

Then a knock, when Claire and Philippe (our grandchildren) stood at our door holding an Easter card for Grandma and a drawing of Christ on the Cross.

26th March 1989

Falling asleep, God revealed Jesus on the cross. Vision small, half usual magnification. A circle of light across Jesus and behind his head. Just above the circle was a child angel.

30th March 1989

Last evening, just before my birthday, God revealed three young children playing. The two youngest girls then the two eldest of our grandchildren. Then Claire and Philippe appeared together (the two youngest). I then fell asleep, for God had revealed our two youngest grandchildren, all four in fact.

In the morning there was a knock at our door, and our four grandchildren (Madeleine, Annette, Claire and Philippe) were standing there holding a birthday card and a book ("Back to the Land") for me. How lovely, I thought. Easter gifts.

5th April 1989

At night, a skeletal form revealed as of an ancient animal, the Devil? It quickly vanished as I called to Jesus and our Father of Love who banished the Devil!

25th April 1989

After reading about King David in the first book of Samuel, I fell asleep. About an hour later to my soul the Lord granted a vision of Africa when a dark Latin cross was laid from the Mediterranean to the Cape. Then the whole of Africa was embraced by the Godhead form and All-Seeing Eye central.

12th May 1989

After reading Kings II at night, our God granted a vision of two male figures: a thin one bent down, and embraced the other and kissed – a call to all to do likewise, I sensed. A Godly concern for men.

13th May 1989

A visiting large ginger cat by day, high up in the branches of the fallen oak in our garden.

15th May 1989

A wild duck flying fast from the west flew low over the site of the crosses towards the east, this morning.

8th June 1989

At night a brimstone ribbon vision moving from west to east in our bedroom was revealed; awake after Bible reading.

12th June 1989

A 'V' formation of thirty to thirty-three geese from the south turned overhead when we were at Barcombe Parish to fly to the east. On the river bank were four Canada Geese we noted (standing by the River Uck at Barcombe). In our garden, wild poppies grew in the form of a square. These, I observed later, were very large and I painted the scene.

7th July 1989

A Latin cross near our bedroom window with oranges growing on the right. Crows flew out from the intersection of a cross. Clouds in the form of Ireland and UK, I noted, by day, in the sky overhead.

9th July 1989

At night after Bible reading, a vision of Mary with Jesus. Below on the floor three or four children were romping about a Church floor, reborn, I sensed?

15th July 1989

A vertical shaft of light in our bedroom window. The top grew into a long arm with the hand reaching down to a smaller hand and arm pointing up but they did not touch each other. Hand of God above, no doubt?

16th July 1989

Sunday. The crucifix above Holy Cross church pulpit glowed at the top only as a sermon was being preached by a Canon. (Again God calls to the church to return to the Bible as the prime source of Grace, no doubt.)

19th July 1989

A vision of a hanging blue flag in the form of an equilateral triangle, blue, in our bedroom after Bible reading.

3rd August 1989

On holiday in Germany, we attended a Hannover Civic Ceremony with our son, which we thoroughly enjoyed.

9th August 1989

At home: huge wild poppies in the form of large signs grew in the shape of SG in our garden. The 'Son of God', 'Saviour God' and 'Sovereign God' was the message we sensed.

13th August 1989

After reading Psalm 136, a huge hand and arm of God in colour was thrust through our bedroom wall from the east to two Bibles at my bedside, low over the 'New King James' and 'Jerusalem Bibles'. UNITY to come?

Then a whole series of hands in the window of visions: A pair grasped a hand pointing forward, one upwards, a palm forward, one of a clenched fist, one pointing to north, one south, one east and one west. To the whole world in fact.

16th August 1989

A robin red sings outside our bedroom window each morning, I have noted.

22nd August 1989

Flower-like groups of lights in houses in New Town, Uckfield, appear each evening, south of our home:

> Peace Peace
> Evolves through
> All-out
> Christian
> Endeavour (God's message to my soul today
> an experience which we may all share in)

12th October 1989

Vision: Jesus on the cross, then the Bride of Christ, in a white dress, on Our Lord's right. Then three crosses in succession revealed, held by the large hand of God. God calling women to the Priesthood?

16th October 1989

A soul vision of Gethsemane. Central was a great stone recessed in the wall when the All-Seeing Eye appeared central in the head-form. To the left was a young child in a knee-length dress with white ankle shoes and socks.

18th October 1989

The last swallows of summer overhead today were diving and circling the branches of an ash, quite close to, and above the site of the crosses, earlier on in the day.

30th October 1989

After reading Jeremiah 48, in the window of visions from Heaven, God revealed the whole of the world as a light grey map. Then Africa, as dark grey, central. Later on, when awake, a pale grey circle with the dark form of the whole of Africa was revealed.

11th November 1989

At 7.30 a.m. my dear sister-in-law, M, spoke to my soul, "Percy." She worships in a Baptist Church in West Sussex and we have sensed that she frequently prays for us both. In East Berlin, this hour of Freedom has arrived. The high dividing wall between East and West Berlin! What a great rejoicing will follow with the growing freedom overall, after the fall.

19th November 1989

This evening there was a blaze of lights again in New Town, Uckfield, England, south of our home.

19th November 1989

A visionary dream of a square box in our vegetable garden. It had been tunnelled under and was partly covered by an old coat with another animal close by? I put my arm in to touch the lamb when I noticed that there lay hidden a young fox! Withdrawing my arm, believing I had trapped the fox, it suddenly shot out of the hole in the ground and raced off.

Three days ago I was granted a visionary dream of a huge flying saucer, it seemed? A huge circular fuel tank central, and above, an engine. Passengers strapped in their seats had a cosmic and earthly view through carved glass all around and doors? The seating was of a circular form. This, I noted, where it was resting on the ground close by our home and bedroom.

God granted a circle of Light on this same site, at the end of the three hour trance, July 18th, 1976.

28 November 1989

I was at work in the garden today when two large white passenger planes from the East, perhaps less than a mile between them in flight, when the first veered to the north, and the other followed. Shortly afterwards a large 'V' formation of white sea birds or wild geese flew overhead from east to west. To their right was a second 'V' formation as it were, flying parallel.

30th November 1989 St Andrew's Day

Today many birds were flying about in the garden, and above our house and the three cross site.

18th December 1989

Vision granted in the night of large black fist holding a dagger pointing downwards over the three Bibles? I called out to Jesus from the soul, believing it to be of the Anti-Christ, when I was filled with the Holy Spirit of God. (For the Devil was troubling me no doubt, as it has done so before in our bedroom of Heavenly night vision.)

20th December 1989

During the night I was granted the golden light of a star a great distance away to the East. Thanking God, then meditating, the star was revealed a second time.

7th January 1990

In the night a vision to my soul of Jesus on the cross in the east, facing west. Then it turned effortlessly facing the south, and then to the north. It was as if the cross was pivoted. Then it was wholly enclosed with a large white but narrow circle of radiant light, the oneness of Christ and our Father God.

Since this experience I cannot accept carved images of Jesus on the cross or of the Virgin Mary carved or of them painted unless the sculptor or artist had first been blessed with a vision by our Creator God. For Jesus has risen indeed.

9th January 1990

Vision: Soldiers in their thousands it appears, 40/46. All seeking freedom today.

15th January 1990

A vision of a white cat and a black cat and then a black and white cat. Then a black/white dog in our garden.

28th January 1990

Two seagulls from the east passed low over the cross site today.

29th January 1990

Early evening, in our bedroom, a figure close to our wardrobe then behind the Bibles. I felt it to be of the Anti-Christ and prayed to Jesus when it vanished. Thanks be to God. Last night a figure in a mackintosh appeared near our wardrobe. Then it appeared by the Bibles as before. Meditating on it being an angel of light, the head turned to a soft golden light when central, there shone forth a golden eye. Ten pigeons appeared on the grass lawn in the morning. Then four wild geese appeared overhead later, from the west, flying to the east and flew now over the three cross site.

30th January 1990

Last night, I dreamt of the River Uck flooding. On 2nd February 1990 the valley was flooded. Perhaps a Revelation of those days when tidal waters covered our valley 8000-10000 years ago or the Waters of Healing to Uckfield today.

2nd February 1990

This morning at 5.45 a.m. I was shaken by a great bang or explosion. Later, I sensed that it was in my soul, from God.

3rd February 1990

Today there appeared a large flock of crows in our beech tree, east of our home.

12th February 1990

After Bible reading: A message to my soul this morning, "Yes."

16th February 1990

Today received message that my dear brother Cyril had died suddenly a few days ago (three?). He had been to see slides of the painted visions on his birthday, 5th November 1989. Then he looked quite serious, but no comment.

5th March 1990

In a dream, when asleep, I was close to bushes and rocks when a large serpent, viper, or snake came writhing towards me and I began beating it when it died. Was it the Devil?

10th March 1990

Today, a brown ladybird appeared on the grasses on the site of three crosses.

A brown spot on my right shoulder has now formed an equilateral dark triangle of dry skin. We believe that Jesus carried the crucifixion cross on the right shoulder.

11th March 1990

I dreamt of a marriage to a young Chinese girl. Recently I sent out seventy-five photocopies of painted visions of China, and trust the day will dawn when they can purchase copies of our *Divine Revelations*.

27th March 1990

Three nights ago God granted a vision of man with a large bushy beard of hair. Then a woman appeared at his side.

30th March 1990

I suddenly recalled that Beth was granted a vision of our Lord about seven days ago in our east bedroom window. He appeared to her to be sitting and talking on the side of a hill. Tomorrow is my birthday, 31st of March.

8th April 1990

The drying skin of stigmata on the back of my right hand today presented a clear image of our Dear Lord. Being only a quarter of an inch across, I examined it with a magnifying glass, when I noted a crown on His headform. 'Amazing Grace', for our Lord scratched the skin on my right hand at the end of the two hour trance, July 18th, 1976.

1st May 1990

Vision of the head of a young girl, twelve to fifteen years of age.

2nd May 1990

The Lord granted a vision of a flowering branch on my right. I had read Numbers 16 in the morning, chapter 17, relating the flowering of Aaron's Branch, from the Bible.

6th May 1990 (soul travel to Holy Cross Church)

Awake, after reading Numbers 27, later God granted a vision of our Lord who appeared blessing Mary Magdelen at his feet in the east coloured windows of Holy Cross Church in Uckfield. The Chancel at each end was revealed and the pulpit on the north side in the Chancel. Then Beth and I listened to a service of Meditation on the Revelations of Dame Julian of Norwich on the radio.

Later God revealed the pulpit in HC again with the crucifix above on the wall. A large Bible lay on the top revealing an arc of spiritual light above it. (Again God's call to return to Bible form of worshipping in the C of E). I informed the Rector several months ago that God had revealed thirteen Bibles ablaze with Light on various dates, the Branches of the 'One True Vine', asking for a return to the Bible form of worship (on thirteen occasions it was confirmed).

7th May 1990

Vision of a large grave, having been excavated and there were three figure-forms with swaths of bandages as of a Shroud. Then on the right was the head form of the 'All-Seeing Eye'. Then I noted the limbs, arms and legs began to move so the bindings broke, it appeared. Later the human form of a woman (in colour) walked from the west side to the east side in our bedroom. She was wearing a brilliant emerald green dress and had coral-colour hair. Did she symbolise Ireland?

Later in the night God revealed what appeared to be a battered figure of a man on the ground.

8th May 1990

This evening we watched the film 'D-Day', the Allied army freeing the French.

12th May 1990

A vision at the edge of a forest. A lioness broke through grasses and brushwood. Then she was revealed lying on her side suckling two cubs, and two or three were romping nearby.

A vision: an excavated grave revealed three draped figures side by side. Slowly the arms and legs of the figures moved then the vision ended. A badly battered body of a human figure (a man) lay motionless on the ground.

22nd May 1990

After reading Joshua, chapter 13, an evil face of Anti-Christ appeared close to my face. Then a grinning face protruding from a crumpled printed newspaper. (God's Revelation?) I then called to God, "Get thee behind me Satan," and the evil vision vanished, whereupon I thanked God.

Today a tree creeper bird settled on an upright post just in front of my face holding a mosquito in its beak, as I walked towards our vegetable garden, close by our stable, "The Chapel of Christ and our Father of Love": confirmed by God to my soul. A future Healing Centre?

31st May 1990

The stigmata on my left wrist in the evening revealed the number seven. In the morning it had changed to three. (Amazing Grace.)

2nd June 1990

A 'painted lady' butterfly appeared on our south terrace, opening and closing its wings slowly.

5th June 1990

Beth experienced a sphere of golden light over her Bible on the left, last night.

20th June 1990

A dream: I had parked outside a greengrocer's shop in Heathfield. Beth was shopping. A female blackbird settled on a box of wrapped south American green guavas. Suddenly it began stripping off the white paper wrappings, and dropping them on to the pavement to blow away. We had just come from visiting a garden open for a charity, in Rusklake Green a few miles away.

29th June 1990

After Bible reading, a vision on the left of Beth of a woman draped in a dress from head to feet as the Muslims wear. It was in pale grey. A few days earlier I had sent seventy-five photocopies of Revelations to the Government and Citizens of Iran, being prompted to do so after the death of several thousand, in a great earthquake there.

At night, to the right in our window of visions there appeared a village street in West Sussex which we were planning to visit tomorrow, a house and high hedgerow and then a circular roundabout road. Then the village street with two or three persons walking close by the old house of my great uncle Philip, I thought, at Sompting, West Sussex.

24th July 1990

After reading chapters I and II of Esther, the Lord granted a vision of a large wagon wheel with wooden spokes and a large hub or crown. It had an iron rim. Out of the crown ran two straight cords, one upwards to Heaven and one to the north. I then fell asleep thinking of farmers and my youth. Was it a revelation that the cord pointing to the north revealed that there is now a link between north and south in the UK?

Today, six gatekeeper butterflies were flying in and out of a periwinkle plant in full bloom and of green foliage. Several more were flying up and out of the surrounding grasses now in seed. I counted twenty-one (seven multiplied by three) here on the site of the three crosses above the three ley line intersections. Thus symbolising our God of all Creation and the Word, and the three of the New and Christ of the Godhead III.

25th August 1990

After reading chapter 9 of Esther, the Lord granted a vision of a woman with white trousers and a green jacket. In the morning a woman appeared in our drive wearing these colours, and she walked away up towards the Pilgrim's Walk, Hempstead Road. I was amazed for the woman was dressed just as the vision revealed.

27th August 1990

At night, a head of an African man granted, then that of an African woman's head.

5th August 1990

After Bible reading at night, a visionary dream of standing on the pavement outside a greengrocer's shop, having picked up a bunch of white grapes to purchase. Then God revealed an African lady standing by who picked up a bunch of black grapes and she said, "Why not buy these?"

13th August 1990

Vision granted of a soldier in khaki holding a gun? Saddam Hussein perhaps, for he was wearing a black beret, as revealed on television. I know not.

18th August 1990

Vision of a vine with white grapes. Shortly afterwards over the Bibles was revealed a man's head wearing a close-fitting cloth cap. Rather like the figure of the Limoges plaque found in our garden beneath the roots of a large oak tree. God had led me there to dig out this thirteenth century plaque which has four holes where it may have been nailed to a wooden cross carried here on this Pilgrim's Way. Thirteenth to fifteenth century? Canterbury – Winchester?

27th August 1990

Vision: Women digging a trench across Lewes crossroads, High Street, by a tobacconist shop, of pre-war days? Then I drove a Morgan three-wheeler, a red car, I recall.

8th September 1990

Four wild ducks flying from the west to east today flew over the site of the crosses.

28th September 1990

A few days' rest in West Sussex. We enjoyed staying for a few days in Lancing Ring Road. At night God granted a vision of three yellow tulips. There then followed a vision to my soul of three red roses. Tomorrow or in fact today is Beth's birthday. A visionary dream of seeing a hole in our garden bank where I was standing with my daughter E. A fox came out and jumped up on to my shoulder so then I called to E to pull its tail and to shake it off which she did. I thus recalled the vision which I was granted of a fox in the well of water in our lawn, in an early vision, then a pigeon or dove in our ancient well.

11th October 1990

Vision of two circles of light on the east bedroom window. The two circles then came together to form a loop and a teddy bear with arms raised appeared in this corner of the window of vision. I feel guided now to write them:

Lead	Peace	God
On	Evolves through	Resurrects
Victorious	All-out	All through
Emmanuel	Christian endeavour	Christ Eternal

The birds are messengers from God, for several (two kestrels, and two hawks, swallows and other birds) appeared over the cross site today. A letter came from our son in Hannover the next day. The birds in the Heavens I have grown to recognise as messengers from God, for they continue to fly above this Holy Acre. (Thanks be to God.)

24th October 1990

Vision: A large lion's head holding a man in his mouth. He was both kicking out his legs and punching out his arms, being trapped, no doubt? But by whom, man or animal?

30th October 1990

Twelve rooks from the south flew above the three cross site and then veered eastwards. Four seagulls from the east flew westwards over the cross site today.

31st October 1990

Last night I was granted a vision of many articles in our old tenant farmhouse at 'Weycroft' Devon. Pottery, boxes, plates, china, pottery, large and small. A live chicken or hen, a small cider/beer keg and drum and wine or cider, in barrels. For three generations my family lived and farmed in this lovely stone manor or Abbey in the fourteenth century.

4th November 1990

Last night I dreamt of a pale blue, plaster washed house where a long deep blue sheet hung down over a window box of yellow primroses.

6th November 1990

At night, after attending Lewes Bonfire celebrations, last night, I was granted a vision of a circular wreath of flowers and above, central, the head of an owl.

24th December 1990

Vision of a leaning Tau cross. The arms then changed to human legs wearing army boots/trousers, then five or six legs were revealed? A vision of a nun followed. What did this convey?

30th December 1990

Soul vision: A white envelope, with a stamp having golden light coming from the edges, appeared over Beth's head. What did this convey?

26th January 1991

Today seven seagulls from the north flew over the three cross site and then over all the tall trees in our garden and finally settled in the highest branches of a tall ash tree for ten minutes or so. A rare experience I thought. They were within a hundred metres or so from the three cross site.

1st February 1991

At night after Bible reading, as usual, God granted a vision now in grey of John Constable's 'Cornfield'. A short time, or a few days later, I was led to paint this. Years ago now, when visiting art museums and galleries in London, I formed the opinion that John Constable's oil sketches were the greatest works of art in our country, true revealers of God's creation.

19th February 1991

A vision of a river or lake. A boat with a man and woman. There was quite a group of swans in the foreground on this river. The man in the boat then held high an axe! Was this a scene on the River Axe, Devon in my childhood days where my grandfather died?

3rd March 1991

At night, after Bible reading, a vision of a gleaming Tau cross. A skull of a human head near the base of the cross. Did it relate to Ireland or the Cross dispossessed in Iraq? I do not know.

18th March 1991

Today our Lombardy poplar at the top was filled with visitors, having six or seven pigeons bending low the topmost branches, calling our attention to Italy no doubt.

A vision of a huge elephant in the window of visions in our bedroom, to my soul, after Bible reading at night.

6th April 1991

Tonight after Bible reading, God granted a lovely vision of a red flower and green foliage, over the Bibles, floating horizontally as it were. What did this symbolise? The red rose of hope. The green foliage of the Eternal Creation, of Ireland's peace to come?

St Mary and John the Baptist vision, St Paul's call for Unity – Ephesians 4 v5, 6

"There is One Lord, One Faith, One Baptism and One God who is the Father of All, overall, through all, and within all."

(Thanks be to God I cry.)

14th April 1991

When at my Brother H, and Sister P's home, Ringmer, recently, for tea, a pied wagtail kept hammering at the small lounge window with its beak for a long time. Then my brother Horace drew the curtain and it flew to the opposite window to hammer at the glass, at Beth and my sister Phyllis. It continued for over one and a half hours when we both left for home.

For three years now Beth has been sending out nationwide small parcels of chocolate gifts and her writings on Healing, and a few photocopies of painted visions.

1st May 1991

The starlings, often in threes, sometimes in fours or in twos, frequently fly over the three cross site.

9th May 1991

Three swallows circled the holy three cross site today, coming from the south. Our annual visitors for the summer.

16th May 1991

After Bible reading, a vision of three large church bells, ringing in the Heavens (starlight, no sound). Today there are many birds visiting our garden singing, and wood pigeons quite frequently fly over here.

25th May 1991

Four swifts circled over the three cross site (Death of Gandhi, India?)

3rd June 1991

After Bible reading at night, God granted to my soul a vision of the whole of Africa, when the states were revealed in various tones of grey.

3rd June 1991

At night, after Bible reading, a vision of Africa, revealing light and dark shades of the various states.

7th June 1991

Two hot air balloons appeared over this Holy Site from the north, in June.

11th June 1991

After Bible reading, a visionary dream of a stone coffin and broken pottery. Site of grass strip of Cocks-footgrass close to the three cross site.

15th June 1991-18th June 1991

Today, I slept on in the morning. At 10 a.m., asleep, I experienced a golden light in my soul on the 18th June, the anniversary of Divine Revelations of St Julian of Norwich, England. For all the Divine Revelations granted here are a Divine continuity of those of St Julian 1373, Norwich, I feel.

3rd July 1991

The pigeons have been called by God to confirm many of the visions. For on the 3rd July 1991, two pigeons from the west flew over the three cross site each holding twigs in their beaks, building the New Church? Husband and wife, Unity. In June and July this year (1991) wild poppies grew up twice normal size in the form of the three crosses, united as One. I painted them shortly afterwards.

13th July 1991

After Bible reading at night, a vision of many garden flowers in various tones of grey, both large and small. Then the scene changed to one of a stage or platform. On the right was a Minister sitting with the Bible at a small table. To the left was another table with a large cake, central.

Below, a few rows of chapel members were revealed. I said to Beth, for we were both awake, "Could this be a vision of an Anniversary Service of celebration of the Baptists?"

16th July 1991

Vision at night of my nephew, Nigel, tossing his young son William to his wife in our bedroom; she, Debs, tossed him back and this continued for a time. William is my second name.

19th July 1991

At night, after Bible reading, twelve to fifteen young cherubs were revealed (the babies were on the ceiling after Bible reading).

20th July 1991

A vision of a mother in a low armchair in front of a window with a baby on her lap. Then a swan or goose thrust its head through the window at the baby.

24th July 1991

I noted that it was due east of the three cross site, and the Celtic bank that the wild poppies had appeared in our garden for the second time in our circular flower garden. The garden was filled with many Song birds giving God the Glory. I painted both of these poppy crosses.

26th July 1991

Evening after Bible reading, God granted to my soul a dark hand and arm thrust through the east wall of our bedroom pointing to the three Bibles at my bedside. The African and coloured people's Love for the Bible, no doubt?

27th July 1991

At 3 p.m. a soul travel vision to see Jesus praying for all upon earth. The God poured thousands of stars towards Our Dear Lord to forma huge Star Cone – Jesus at the apex, Amazing Grace, praying for all.

27th July 1991

Four pigeons formed a huge triangle open over the three cross site!

After Bible reading God granted a map in grey of the northern half of the world.

9th August 1991

Asleep in my chair, God granted a vision – so human-like – of my son-in-law, Morgenne, who walked past our east lounge window wearing a long grey coat. At this time he was in Ashdown Forest, walking with his wife and family. Morgenne was both born and educated in Mauritius. He was in fact in the vision walking towards our small stable. One night a few years ago now, God spoke to my soul, "The stable is to be called the chapel of Christ and our Father of Unity Love." (Godhead III). We decided to surrender our home, stable, garden and paddock for a 'Healing Centre', Holy Cross Day, 1978. (At the rebirth of the Church in Unity by the year of 2000 years of Christ , it may become a Healing Centre of Worship. We hope so.)

One sacrifice for all, One church of Unity of Three: (For Jesus said, "I did not come to judge the world, but to save the world." John 12, v 47) "Obey the Truth in purifying your souls, Love one another with sincere brotherly Love."

Love (Advent 1991)

Love once again came to us at night, on the eve of Advent, for we were awake when you Dear God, sent us a glorious luminous human marble-like vision of Mary, the dear Mother of our Lord, after reading the word. Mary, seated with the baby, John the Baptist, unclothed on her left knee. John with his right hand held high, a Latin cross, pointing to the Heavens, to the Father of all Love and source of all Light and Truth and the Word. We were awake when at first, a small circle of light appeared over three Bibles to my right out of which grew the vision of Mary and John, soul magnification.

Oh what Joy was shed upon us all, for this scene, magnified, revealed three persons, though one, our Lord, as yet unborn but no, this cannot be? Yet his Love for us shone through Mary's loving eyes and smile. Mary revealed the Light of Joy, Love, Peace and humility within and without, as she contemplated John, and Jesus, God's new born Son smiling, perhaps upon the floor? It pleased God to reveal Mary and baby John as humans, as with our Lord's head in the tomb (1976).

The three were of one and one of three, for truly God sent the prophet John to Elizabeth to proclaim the Saviour of the world and man, and Mary His chosen One, head of all Saints I see. Jesus who lived as man, died, and rose again for all, His loving ones to see, both then and now, lives on, in the Godhead overall. Mary's Song to Elizabeth "My soul magnifies the Lord..." has been manifested in all the visions granted for they have been magnified through the spiritual Eye of God, grace to the soul. Such Love, I feel transcends all human thoughts and action.

O Saviour of the world come soon and rescue us through your Holy Word, from all our dreadful sin and worldly shame, a call to stand up for 'Truth and Justice'. You came to us two thousand years ago in Love, yet Man rejected you dying upon the cross. Help us O Lord through the Unity of Love, Repentance, Renewal and Revelation to live again in You, and You in us. Help us to pray to Christ and the Father of Love as One in Unity of loving three. The Godhead III of Love and Unity worldwide for all to see.

You, dear Lord, have never failed to Love us, or ever fail to share in all Creation, all life on earth, and in the Glory of the Universe. Born free as a radiant living butterfly, flitting from flower to flower, on wings of sunshine floating upon the sun-drenched air of an English garden in June, free as angels of light supreme, for all around I see your wings of Love. For many birds fly singing over the three cross site or circle over head day by day. Some fly east to west or west to east, north to south or south to north, forming Heavenly crosses of Love, your Light Divine, Eternal.

Here in God's garden home your Light surrounds us both by day and night. All your flowers of colour and light, shrubs, trees and birds on the wing, praise you from sunrise to sunset. Only they give you worthy praise of change from "Glory into Glory" of life renewed again, of life reborn of Love from God to man and man to God supreme. Through Christ is the Way, the Truth and the Life of Unity to come. The Eternal Glory of the Godhead III for all upon the earth.

Jesus you ascended to the Father from whence you came with the promise, "I will come again." For three days after the vision of Mary, your Mother, and John the Baptist the Father revealed to us You in Glory, floating on a bank of white clouds in the blue cosmos. It was evening, when we were awake, you sent us a colour ray of light which touched the ceiling. One cloud of Light. The cloud parted into cloudlets revealing Christ in Glory in a white robe and crowned with a golden crown, radiant with light, floating in a pale blue starlit sky towards the east on a horizontal plane. We feel this foretold your Second Coming one day, foretold by God Our Father of Love. Amazing Grace.

8th April 1992

At 1 a.m., early morning, God granted a vision, dark grey, of the whole of Africa. Central was a small state revealed as light grey. Then the large hand and arm of God (light) pointed to this light grey state of the Central African Republic. Then slowly it was withdrawn, as the vision ended. Then I recall God laying a Latin cross upon the whole of Africa, from the Mediterranean to the Cape. Then the whole of Africa was embraced by the Godhead form. I painted this glorious scene of light.

Since 16th June 1973, after Bible reading by day, God has granted over twice as many Revelations of God's Creation than of visions to my soul at night, bird flight phenomena over almost nineteen years has been most active over the site of three crosses close to our small stable here. Some circle over, some fly E-W or W-E. Others N-S or S-N.

I may have written this revelation of the cross upon Africa earlier on and I sent copies to the president and the government?

27th July 1992

Resting at 3 p.m. God again revealed to my soul Jesus in Glory, at the apex of a Radiant Star-cone! Praying for us all upon earth. However no stars were revealed in the Universe on this occasion, only the radiant star-cone Amazing Grace. Thus God revealed Jesus in Glory for the second occasion as foretold in Psalm 33, v 13, 14 and 15.

"Yahweh looks down from Heaven, He sees the whole human race. From where he sits and watches all who live on the earth. He who moulds every heart and takes note of all they say and do."

> Christians
> Hear the
> Royal call in
> Glory:
> Salvation
> To all Mankind

Thus the Divine message to my soul in mid-February 1974 when a huge circle of seagulls appeared overhead from the west and on looking Heavenwards, God spoke to my soul, "I Am the One Church in the One World in the One Universe" (God in all Creation and the Word revealed, Unity, Now and in Eternity).

God's call to all mankind to return to the Bible for therein lies the prime source of Grace and Unity of all branches of the 'One True Vine' as foretold by Jesus, "I am the Vine, ye are the branches."

In June and July this year of 1992 the wild poppies again grew up rapidly, twice normal size in the form of a large 'S' and a 'G' = Son of God, Saviour God, and Sovereign God. They were intermingled with wild white marguerites.

Extract from our Diary of Discovery and Revelation

Sat 9th May 1992 (from September 1978)

Recently I have been led to read through our diary in order to list the growing Revelations to my soul of the country of Africa: this diary was recorded from 15th June 1973, the first Revelation of God's Creation and the word revealed, on the 600th anniversary of the Divine Revelations of St Julian of Norwich, England, June 15th 1973.

To return to the Bible: **Revelations 22, v 9**

"The Angel said to John, 'I am a servant just like you, and like your brothers the prophets, and like those who treasure what you have written in this book (Bible). It is God you must worship.'"

Rev 22, v 4

They will see Him face to face, and His name will be written on their forehead.

God has confirmed this (18.7.76) and the mark of the † on my forehead is clearly visible now. On my right shoulder, where Jesus carried the cross, God has marked it thus: a brown hard skin patch revealing just a spot of Our Dear Lord's suffering for all mankind. We all thank you for your amazing Love for all mankind throughout the Nations of the World and we look forward to your Second Coming in Glory.

For Jesus thus promised us the future oneness and Glory of the church in Unity to come before He rejoined our Father God in Heaven on Resurrection Day. Confirmed through the four all glorious Godhead visions granted here on this Holy Cross Acre over the past twenty-one years and more.

For there are many unanswered questions we have all to face in life. Those we have Loved are suddenly taken to where, we may ask? I can only share with all mankind the experiences of the Eternal Glory granted to us here over the years after Bible reading night and morning, the Glory of the visitation of our Dear Lord Jesus, 11 p.m. 21st March 1986, after reading one verse, John 14, v 21. The granting of over seventy Divine visions at night after Bible reading of the Old and New Testaments night and morning, of the Glory of the Unity of Christ and our Father God Creator in the Oneness of the Godhead III. The Church reborn in Unity by the end of 2000 years of Christ and the dawn of the Godhead third millennium – Godhead III. (This I have written before, I am sure. Please forgive me.) Yet our Dear Lord in Glory has granted at least 200 Divine Revelations.

Job said, "Oh that I knew where I could find Him." (Job 23, v 3) (Ezekiel 18, v 4) foretold this age, "For all have sinned and come. short of the Glory of God, there is none righteous, no not One." For all the World is guilty before God." (Romans 3, v 19.) Man's only saviour is Christ alone who unlocks the gates of the One with the golden key of Heaven.

This is through Christ to God the Father of all, the All-Glorious Godhead III of now and in Eternity. Amazing Love.

'Thy will be done' for Jesus said:

"Thou shalt Love the Lord thy God with all they heart and with all thy soul, and with all thy mind, and with all thy strength. This is the first commandment and the second... thou shalt Love thy neighbour as thyself. There is none other commandment greater than these."

And so God confirmed his Son in Glory at 3 p.m., to my soul, when I fell asleep on 27th July 1991. Jesus, one with God our Father Creator of the whole Universe, the earth and all mankind. Jesus was revealed in the stars praying. Then God opened the Universe, pouring thousands of brilliant stars to form a huge Star-cone around our Dear Lord, Jesus at the apex. (This I have mentioned before, but such glory is ever with us.)

This Amazing Grace was confirmed again twelve months later, in 1992, and for the third occasion in Glory, last March 27th 1993 after evening Bible reading, just before my birthday. With the Revelation in 1992 and 1993, Jesus was revealed at the apex of the Star-cone, praying as he looked down upon the whole earth, through God's Star-cone of Light! Again, amazing Grace.

31st March 1993 (my birthday)

"Glory is our destiny"

Read: Romans 8, v 18-19

"I think that what we suffer in this life can never be compared with the Glory, as yet unrevealed, which is waiting for us."

This is through Christ to God the Father of all, the all glorious Godhead III of now and in eternity. For Jesus did appear here in our lounge on 21st March 1986 after reading John 14, v 26. Amazing Love and Grace, at 11 p.m. that evening.

"Thy will be done" for Jesus said, 'Thou shalt Love the Lord thy God with all thy heart and with all thy soul, and with all thy strength', this is the first commandment and the second... thou shalt Love thy neighbour as thyself. There is none other commandment greater than these."

And so God confirmed his Son in Glory surrounded by stars at 3 p.m., to my soul after I fell asleep on 27th September 1991. Jesus, One with God our Father Creator of the whole Universe the earth and all mankind. The Spirit revealed to me again at the third hour, to witness our Dear Lord at the apex of a cone of radiant stars.

This Amazing Grace was confirmed again twelve months later, and for the third occasion, in Glory, last March 27th 1993 after evening Bible reading just before my birthday.

How I long to share all of Our Dear Lord God's Divine Revelations with all mankind throughout the world and in the universe. I hope that *Divine Revelations* may be of some help. God bless.

31st March 1993

So that which I have been searching for, for some seventy-seven years now, I was never able to find in Anglican forms of worship but only in the Nonconformist Bible-loving chapels and churches for the revealed word of God then is pre-eminent, transcending all institutional forms of worship, yet Love is the key – Unity of Love.

"Thy will be done."

The oneness of Jesus and our Father God Creator.

(Reader, I apologise for the repetition you may find from time to time.)

Last evening we were watching television about 8 p.m. when a blackbird flew into the east window of our lounge, pecking the glass and beating its wings. I got up and noted, just as another blackbird appeared just below the window, with a nine inch length of dried grass in its beak to be used for building a nest. On a number of occasions this year and a few times in the past a blackbird has flown against the lounge window and against the large east window of our sun loggia leaving a mark on the double glazing! In fact I recall that at least two have died here in the past! Later on, I recall appealing to the Wealden DC and the County Councils to provide a home for the 'Weycroft

Collection' of watercolours and the large collection of carved stones from this Holy Acre. We, living here, know that God uses his created birds daily on this Holy Acre to confirm the 'healing visions' granted here. This year for the first time since the 'Great Storm', autumn 1987, the thrushes and a larger mavis have nested here in our garden and in the paddock hedgerows. They also come to sing each morning and evening perched on the roof of our stable overlooking the three cross site below in the grass at the eastern end of the stable. For they symbolise the black and the brown people being raised in Africa, India, etc, we feel.

The black birds no doubt confirm God's revelations concerning the coloured nations and Africa being 'raised up', nationwide. The thrushes and mavis confirm the message on the three cross site: "the east shall first link with the west, (England, Wales, Ireland) then the North with the South". Scotland with southern England and Wales? Also perhaps Northern Ireland with southern Ireland is God's will? Ref.: the (T) Tau cross of grass revealed on 15th June 1990 when the left arm grew into a map of Ireland and the other two arms into a map of England, Wales and Scotland. Finally, over six weeks the grass grew into a perfect dark green circle.

15th June 1993

The Divine Revelations commenced here with the appearance of three concentric circles of seagulls flying in a perfect clockwise direction, on a horizontal plane from the west, about midday 1973. The Power and the Glory of our loving Godhead III continues and will do so until the end of 2000 years of Christ, and the dawn of the third millennium Godhead III. The dawn of the Christian Church reborn in Unity (For the symbol of three has ever been with me, from my birth at Weycroft, Axminster, Devon, our tenant farmhouse home, on 31 March 1916).

(An ancient home of first Catholic worship, and then Non-conformist Axminster Congregational worship.) Then Anglicans, I believe, followed? Foretelling UNITY, I feel.

Tuesday 6th July 1993

On Saturday evening, after Bible reading, God granted a vision of a bonny baby of at least twelve months of age, lying in his cradle. Last eve, again after Bible reading, in our bedroom I was granted a vision of a mother, so tired it appeared, who had fallen asleep in a winged armchair holding a book or Bible between her knees. To the left on the floor was the bonny baby now asleep.

Again this summer there have been a variety of the lovely wild butterflies. Once again, close to the three cross site, the 'gatekeepers' have been most evident.

August 1993

For Jesus said, "Where two or three are gathered together, there am I in their midst." The end of 2000 years of Christ and the dawn of the Godhead III of the third millennium. Thanks be to God.

Last eve, we both listened to a programme on television concerning ill-treatment of children, used for sexual practices, by the priesthood in the Church in the USA.

Friday July 9th 1993

This eve, listening to the news on TV, we suddenly heard a bang on the east window of our sun loggia. I quickly went to see and there was a large woodpecker flat out on the grass below with a lovely red head of feathers and coloured back and wings, slowly opening and closing its eyes. Beth brought a glass of water as I had asked her to, then I sprinkled its head, praying to God.

It then opened its eyes and twice its long tongue came out from its beak. Again I sprinkled more water and asked God for its healing.

And so, after about ten minutes of forced rest, it stood on its legs and moved a foot or so, looking directly at us.

Quite suddenly, it flew up and off to our garden and the trees in the east and called twice to us, later on. At Saturday lunch time, it was raining, when two woodpeckers flew close by our kitchen window N-S. Husband and wife, I thought. A flight of thanks! Answer to my prayer. Today I read Isaiah 45, v 22, "Look unto me and be saved... I am God."

14th July 1993

Our nephew David and Rebecca called for a coffee this morning staying until 12.30 a.m. In early August they set out for Hong Kong and China, in the mission field. I had declared a number of the Divine Revelations to them.

Last night after Bible reading I was granted a vision of a staff, as it were, held over Beth by the Holy Spirit for it was leaning towards me with the head of the staff above my head.

Beth called to God, I felt, on parallel lines, God's confirmation of our working for the rebirth of the Church of Unity of Love.

18th July 1993

Last eve, or during the night I again called out, "Police, Police, Police." A repetition of once a year since we have lived here for almost thirty-eight years now. I have informed the local police of many of the Revelations granted from God.

16th August 1993

Following Bible reading last eve, and falling asleep, God granted a vision of a woman's head. Today I felt that it may have been St Julian of Norwich, but it was so brief. Then my soul received this message: "Do not worry for money will be forthcoming." A few weeks ago I applied for a publisher to print a portion of our meditations and extracts from our diary of discovery and revelations. It may have to wait until 1994 or late 1995. Perhaps *Divine Revelations* may be the title?

20th August 1993

A reply has come, but no offer to publish the diary of 'Discovery and Revelations'. Perhaps the publication of photos of the painted visions should come first. I have to be patient, no doubt. Time will tell.

The birds have continued daily to confirm God's message on the three cross site here by our stable, God's call: "The stable is to be called the chapel of Christ and our Father of Love," i.e. "The east shall first link with the west, then the north with the south," by the end of 2000 years?

28th August 1993

After Bible reading an Angel of Light had appeared at the end of our bed. Earlier in the evening a lady had telephoned to say that she had attended a Council meeting where the subject under discussion was related to the erection of a building on our land, I replied that God had already revealed that our stable is to be called 'The Chapel of Christ and our Father of Love'. To be reconstructed on the site of our old stable, a future 'Healing Centre' no doubt? Perhaps the Church reborn at the end of the 2000 years Christ Age?

23rd August 1993

After Bible reading at night God granted a vision of four large circular biscuits in our bedroom, also the long arm and hand of God over the light and three Bibles at our bedside. This then I believe is the fourteenth Revelation from God calling attention to the Bibles.

That all Branches are called to return to a Bible form of worship, thus establishing the 'One church of Love' of the Godhead III of Grace and the Healing of divisions: one church of Love is Unity by AD2000. For we approach the third millennium age with the church reborn in Unity at the end of 2000 years of Christ.

This morning I read Daniel 9 and commenced 'The Great Vision' Daniel 10. The apparition of an Angel – for here is a new vision about these days – it is to tell you about the 'Book of Truth' about these things – the 'Souths with the Norths'. (Thus I recalled one of the 6 messages to my soul on the site of God's three crosses † T +. "The east shall first link with the west, then the north with the south."

Chapter 12, "Michael will stand up – there is going to be a time of great distress!" (This I feel has already begun).

I am thus led to recall the two hour trance, Jesus Head wrapped in the napkin of the tomb, eyes ablaze with light, three messages to my soul at the end:

1. "Stand down from all institutions of man."
2. "My soul being advanced to the end of the 'Christ Age'."
3. "Communicate the experiences to all nations."

Thus foretelling the end of 2000 years of Christ and the dawn of the Godhead, third millennium: Unity.

August 1993

Again this summer there have been a variety of the lovely wild butterflies. Once again close to the three cross site the gatekeepers have been most evident.

For Jesus said, "Where two or more are gathered together, there am I in their midst." The end of 2000 years of Christ and the dawn of the Godhead III of the third millennium.

Thanks be to God, and his Amazing Love, I cry.

21st August 1993

Last night I was troubled after a friend had telephoned enquiring whether I was going to erect a building on this Holy Acre. I replied, "No, for we have committed our home and garden, a paddock of two acres of this Holy Acre to our Godhead III for a Healing centre." When the branches of the Church have united by the end of 2000 years of Christ.

Later, after Bible reading last night, God granted an angel of light standing at the end of our bed. God's answer to my prayer. No wings were revealed, as history reveals. Although they were in a vision of Mary kneeling and praying at the foot of the cross in a past revelation.

9th September 1993

After Bible and psalm reading in the night, God once again granted a vision of the long arm and hand of God, thrust through the east wall of our bedroom over the Bibles at our bedside. In the hand was now revealed a piece of ore or sandstone? Such as I have brought into our house recently after weeding a circular flower border on the eastern side of our drive. Many hundreds of carved pieces of stone have been collected here in our garden over the years. (This was the circular flower garden where the red poppies grew into the three crosses. As reported earlier).

For all the carved stones revealed here over the years we believe had been carved by man up to 8,000-10,000 years ago. Guided by God no doubt. For this Celtic bank, site of the three crosses, was partly excavated by the former owner, and before in-filling it after purchase, I noted a large pile of minute flint chippings, some four feet six inches to five feet below the turf, on the surface. I collected a number of carved flints. For this must have been occupied by man 10,000 years ago, I feel.

23rd September 1993

Last eve, after Bible reading, a vision of four circular biscuits in our bedroom. Yesterday God granted a beautiful brilliant rainbow over the sunshine over this Holy Acre. A high arch over this site where Mary and the Christ child appeared. It lasted about one to two hours I recall. Later on there was a brilliant flash of lightning and a great bang of thunder over Manor Park, on the north side of Hempstead Lane, Pilgrims Way.

28th September 1993

Last night, after Bible reading, I experienced a visionary dream of our son crying, sitting beside a man we know, on our settee, close by the site where Jesus appeared on 21st July 1986, in our lounge. Concerning men no doubt, God revealed two, side by side. Healing will be granted one day.

A day later I was crying after listening to a well known man on TV evensong, who was reading from the Bible. He has the same Christian name, I believe, as my son Clive.

5th October 1993

This afternoon we were again granted a beautiful rainbow high arched, right over the cobnut bush where the Virgin Mary appeared holding the Christ child, in a photo slide of our garden taken late March 1988. Yet this vision was not revealed to my soul (the wonder and Glory of God), it was revealed on a colour slide photo which I had taken of the Spring garden blossoms.

Last eve, after Bible reading, God granted a colour natural vision of my head looking forward. This morning I wondered, am I to draw or paint my head? Or did it indicate God's call to work for future Revelations?

The Very Revd. Pope John Paul II, last eve, declared the Catholic Faith: for myself it is predestination from birth over seventy-seven years ago. Reading our Bible both night and morning is of great help for it is God's call to all branches of the One True Vine. For when reading it, God reveals the Truth to our souls. "Thy Will be Done." God's amazing Love.

18th October 1993

We returned from a very restful holiday with C, our Son, in Sheepfold Road, Guildford this evening.

God one night granted a vision of light over our bed. Two nights ago after Bible reading at night, a vision of an Angel of light to my soul was revealed over Beth on a horizontal plane. There was a white frost last evening but the red fuchsias are blooming still in our garden.

28th October 1993

Last evening God granted Beth a vision of a beautiful spray of pale blue flowers.

29th October 1993

Last eve, after Bible reading, God granted a vision of a yellow flower and shortly afterwards that of a white flower. By the garden three white roses are in full bloom today close to the site of the three crosses.

7th November 1993

Sunday evening I listened to a service of singing and prayer in which Cliff Richard was reading the Bible, and also singing hymns of praise. I cried for it was but a day or two ago that I had been granted a sad vision of my son C, crying and sitting in a settee in our lounge beside another C. What was God revealing, I thought, here in the room where Jesus appeared on 21st July 1986?

Trees and shrubs have been shedding their lovely garments of many colours. On Saturday evening our family enjoyed our annual bonfire and fireworks. Beth, Clive, Elizabeth and two friends helped with food and drinks.

The sky was frequently filled all around with bursting sky rockets and flowering colour sprays. Next day, honeybees by the dozen were collecting by day both nectar and pollen from our hedgerow ivy bush. God has indeed blessed us all with his glorious Heavenly sunshine after several weeks of heavy rain.

11th November 1993

Last night after Bible reading God granted a vision of a sad and mentally ill man. Then a vision of a woman appeared in yellow Shortly after I was granted a vision of a woman dressed in pinkish-red and then a third one, dressed in white. They then appeared walking towards the west in our bedroom. They confirm the yellow and red flowers that appeared earlier, no doubt?

To date, our Godhead III of Love, has granted over one hundred and seventy recorded visions and Revelations after Bible reading, both night and morning. In fact, over some eighteen years, I have read the Bible completely through twelve times over, reading both by night and in the morning. Thanks be to God.

By day we have been granted over three hundred and forty confirmations of the visions through the call of God's Creation. Especially, bird flight phenomena over and above the three cross site by the chapel for the stable is to be called the 'Chapel of Christ and our Father of Love'. Flowers, plants, trees, butterflies, bushes, etc., were especially revealed confirming God's call. For this is the name given to our Stable by God for a future 'Healing Centre' of 'Love in Unity' (One Church). 'The Chapel of Christ and our Father of Love.'

NB: Revelations III, v 13

"He who has an ear, let him hear what the 'Spirit' is saying to the churches."

II Peter 3, v 9.

"The Lord is not too slow in keeping His promise, as some understand slowness. He is patient with you, not wanting anyone to perish but everyone to come to Repentance."

(Photocopies sent to SA Government and to Archbishop D. Tutu and family after the vision ceased. My apologies for the few lines added after I had sent a copy to the SA Government.)

13th November 1993

On looking out of our kitchen window this morning, foretelling the 'Remembrance Day Service' at St Margaret's with the Queen yesterday at Buxted, my friend the woodpecker appeared on the lawn picking up fallen leaves and stacking them. Rebuilding the church in Unity, I thought, many colours, many nations?

The woodpecker then flew into a nearby conifer pecking at the branches. Shortly afterwards it flew over our Celtic garden to a Scots pine, settling on a branch – rebuilding the church of the One Godhead III to come north to south, I thought?

Sunday 28th November 1993

Last night God granted a vision of my late dear mother, Florence May. She was walking towards me dressed in a white pinafore dress as of her youth, on the way down to help with the milking in the cowsheds, at Langtye, Ripe.

It has been our second cold week and the seagulls continue to come from the west, settling or wheeling above the community college playing field just across the Pilgrims' Way. On various occasions one could be seen flying over the three cross site, north to south, or south to north. On Wednesday one passed quite low overhead and called out to me as I looked Heavenwards for I was hedgecutting at the time, in our garden.

20th November 1993

This evening I read the 'minor prophets' (twelve in fact from the period of 700 years BC). Thus I was led to recall the 'Birth of Christ' in the vision of the trefoil:

(1) Mary with Jesus, the Christ-child.
(2) Anne with a child central.
(3) Elizabeth with John the Baptist.

Also the vision of Christ's birth, a child Angel looking up to Jesus on Mary's lap and Joseph standing behind.

In this trefoil vision, Jesus only was revealed wholly of Light sitting on Mary's lap with his legs and arms and hands pointing forward. Suddenly He punched out his legs, hands and arms sideways! Amazing Grace. Perhaps foretelling the oneness of the Godhead III at the end of 2000 years of Christ? A call for all to be concerned with working for the Unity of the 'One church of Love' by the end of 2000 years of Christ.

30th November 1993

Today it has turned much milder and is almost 50°F at 10 a.m. Many birds can be seen in our garden.

6th December 1993

Last evening after Bible reading an evil-looking head of the Devil with a huge gaping mouth appeared before me. I cried out to our Lord, and crossed myself, "Get thee behind me Satan" – and the head vanished. From time to time, I have been troubled by the Devil throughout almost twenty-four years of 'Divine Revelations'.

7th December 1993

In the late afternoon, a female blackbird crashed into our sun loggia window, wings on the grass outstretched. I rushed to get a cup of water and whilst praying to God I dripped it slowly on its head. Beth again brought a second cup and as I was praying it opened its eyes and then it finally stood up. As I stroked it, it began to walk a little and then flew off calling to me. The third bird to be restored on this Holy Acre by our God of Love and Creator this year.

For after thirty-seven years of Divine Revelations here my faith is now rooted in the wonder and the Glory and oneness our Godhead III of Love. God in the Glory and beauty of all Creation and the Word revealed. In fact the Church reborn in Unity by the end of 2000 years of Christ. The One church of Love of the Godhead III of the third millennium.

13th December 1993

An American lady, one time in the past a tenant, with her academic husband and family lived next door. Today we received a card for Xmas enclosing a ten dollar gift to help us with sending our cards etc., nationwide. This morning three seagulls called to me over the site of the three crosses, half an hour later a large flock from the north calling loudly attracted my attention.

This evening I read Habukkuk 2, v 11 then Yahweh answered and said, "Write the vision down; inscribe it on tablets to be easily read."

Zachariah 6, 8th, vision the chariots. "Red horses to the east, black horses in the north, the white to the west and the piebald to the south."

NB: for on the three cross site God said, "The east shall first link with the west, then the north with the south."

16th December 1993

After three days of heavy snow (four inches here) there was a sudden thaw last night.

1st January 1994

Matthew 16:

"And the people who lived in darkness have seen a great light! On those who dwell in the land and shadow of death, a light has dawned!"

From that time on Jesus began to preach, "Repent ye for the kingdom of Heaven is at hand."

"Yes," I cry, "for Jesus has now been revealed in Glory three times, praying for us all to return to the Bible, to seek healing and the loving Unity of the Godhead III."

1st January 1994

Yesterday, quite a number of Songbirds returned to our garden to sing on the eve of the new year 1994. A Song thrush (mavis) stayed for a long period singing in our neighbour's apple tree. The owners are of Scottish-Irish descent, I believe.

3rd January 1994

Last evening after Bible reading New Year's Eve, God granted a human-like vision of my dear departed brother. Cyril's head. It was so bright and clear for he died but a few years ago, early in 1990 I recall. There have been very few visions granted in human-colour, as it were. Cyril read our family Bible regularly I believe, as did our dear Grandmother, on Father's side, from Dorset (Frampton).

4th January 1994

This morning once again the River Uck is in full flood.

About 11 a.m. I noted a very large flock of seagulls flying quite low for some three to five minutes from the south and they then flew over our stable, and three cross site, and our home, towards the north.

7th January 1994

This afternoon a large flock of rooks flew over the cross site from south to north.

8th January 1994

Mr Badger, during the night, has been digging up the turf beneath the Scots pine three square yards or so. Guided by God I feel, for but a few days ago I sent off three pages of the history of Divine revelations to the church of Scotland in Edinburgh to share with all branches of the One True Vine.

11th January 1994

Yesterday quite a large flock of seagulls appeared circling and weaving and calling loudly over the site of the three crosses. We have experienced river flooding in the valleys of Sussex for several days now; Chichester and the cathedral have almost been surrounded by flood water and it has been pumped from the streets for several days now, I gather.

25th January 1994

Last night I experienced the mark of the lamb on the back of my right hand: a 'P', Dark red in colour.

28th January 1994

A recent vision was of my niece Katrina standing close by the Bibles on my right. She is married to Luke and they farm in the South of France, south west of Paris, I believe.

Jesus on the shore at the Sea of Galilee was not recognised by Peter and others who went out into a boat fishing and caught nothing. Jesus called out, "Throw the net out to starboard," and the net was filled and other Disciples pulled the net of fish and the boat in to shore. Simon Peter then emptied out the net, having caught one hundred and fifty-three fish (a number divisible by three). They took bread and fish cooked on a fire given to them by Jesus. This was the third time that Jesus had revealed himself to them after the Resurrection. God has revealed Jesus to my soul from Heaven on three occasions now.

Three times Jesus asked Simon Peter, "Do you love me more than these others?" "Yes," he replied each time; again the symbol of three (thus the symbol of three which has been with me throughout life is once again confirmed in the Bible).

I now feel that the time is approaching when we should publish the history of the Divine Revelations and perhaps the photographs later on?

May God bless and guide the readers of this history of Divine revelations for they are a continuation of those of St Julian of Norwich, 1373.

30th January 1994

At night I was granted a vision of two white arms with clenched fists pointing towards me. I cried out to God and they vanished. Yesterday (Saturday) 30th, Clive, our son, came down from Guildford for the day to help plant about thirty young saplings – laurels, thorns (a few) and a yew – on the west boundary of our paddock. This is the boundary which our neighbours, a property development company, destroyed some four or five years ago now. I have been slowly replanting from saplings growing in our one and a half acre paddock, provided by God, it would appear. We do not have to purchase any for these are laurels, thorn, beech, oak, ash, yew, blackthorn etc. This I noted that the mark on the back of my right hand 'P' has now changed to a dark 'G' with the upright arm of the P almost faded, for God is One, One loving Godhead of now and in Eternity.

31st January 1994

This morning the 'G' has taken on the shape of thirteen, on my left arm. Here on this Holy Acre, God granted this lovely prayer of 'Love', in fact, on my late mother's birthday, on 27th January 1994:

> "There is a Light more bright than the midday sun, or the moon and stars by night,
> For it is the Light of Him who Loves us
> All as One,
> One Holy Church of Love."

Thus, these lovely words covered almost twenty-one years of Divine Revelations on this Holy Cross Acre.

3rd February 1994

Evening, after Bible reading, a vision of three white circles close together. There followed a vision of Africa/India – not very clear, a coloured people, no doubt, not clearly understood. Or could this signify a growing fellowship between the UK and Africa and India?

8th February 1994

Vision of a medium brown head of a man either from South India or a state in Africa?

10th February 1994

Evening after Bible reading, there was a flash of light then a woman stood with arms outstretched and a man on the right also with arms out from his sides, both welcoming me? Then a cup or goblet of wine appeared. The church reborn, in Unity, I felt.

This evening as I came into tea about 5.30 p.m. a large brown barn owl swept low overhead, flying north to south then over the three cross site towards the trees beyond our garden. About 5.45 p.m. I looked out over our stable (The chapel of Christ and our Father of Love) and noted a very unusual sight of crows, seven in fact, flying silently over the three cross site south to north, here in the form of an arrowhead. How wonderful God is in granting us the wonder and Glory of His Creation. Romans III v 15, 16, 17, 18. This formation of crows suggested the growing unity of the south with the north in the world?

21st February 1994

Sunday. News that Bosnia has ceased shelling and surrendered all their guns to the UN.

"Their feet are swift when blood is to be shed, wherever they go there is havoc and ruin. They know nothing of the way of Peace, there is no fear of God before their eyes." This I read this evening before going to sleep, a letter from St Paul, from the Bible.

The weather is cold and dull now.

1st March 1994

Morning. Beth, who was watching the cock pheasant and the ginger cat in our garden, noted the pheasant stood his ground and looked the cat in the eyes, when it turned and walked away.

Yesterday was St David's Day.

I thought that it was but a few years ago when I also saw a white cat looking at a cock pheasant at the bottom of our garden. It also turned away and walked off, away from the pheasant.

4th March 1994

This morning Madeleine, Beth's sister, and her daughter Janice came to take Beth with them on a shopping trip to Eastbourne. Just before lunch two sparrowhawks came hovering over our paddock and then flew east over the three cross site.

Earlier this morning seven seagulls from the north appeared over the three cross site hovering around over the cross site for a time. A growing link between the north with the south, I thought.

7th March 1994

A lifetime of searching for reality, end of January 1994. Several weeks ago now, after Bible reading, I received this beautiful poem to my soul, Revelation of a lifetime of Divine Revelations granted to us in late January:

The Unity Foretold, prayer (late January 1994)

There is a light more bright than the midday sun
Or the moon and stars by night
For it is the light of Him
Who Loves us all as One
One Holy church of Love.

My dear mother's birthday was on the 27th January I recall.

In fact, this Godly prayer confirms twenty-one years of Divine Revelations.

Today three wild ducks from the east came over the three cross site and circled and then flew back to the east. Later a single duck from the west circled and flew on to the east. The 'three in one' or 'one in three', I thought.

(The crows were directed by God on Ash Wednesday on 16th February 1994, I thought).

18th March 1994

(A 'V' formation foretelling healing in Bosnia by the night of Sunday 20th, I felt.)

Paul's epistle to the Romans 8, v 25-30, Paul.

Women priests? C16, v 1-16 (Phoebe a deaconess of the church who has looked after many people.)

'The Empire Lives On'

A vision last night, of the whole of the UK and Ireland, each of changing tones of grey.

Today, at 3 p.m. there appeared an ageing fox at the bottom of our garden. As I looked at it, it then turned away and walked off.

The Empire Lives On (extract from our weekly papers)

Mrs Fay Clayton and Mrs Sarah Cullen (right), judging a gymkhana at the Highgate Summer Show near Pietermaritzberg, South Africa. There were thirty-three young entrants and they were all English-speaking whites. "This is the last outpost of the British Empire," says Mrs Clayton. "We are terribly British in this part of the world." Indeed, in Pietermaritzberg itself, the Victoria Club still proudly flies the Union Jack.

There are at least 350,000 British passport holders resident in South Africa. Recently the South African government made it easier for them to obtain a South African passport while keeping their original citizenship, thus making it possible for them to vote in the forthcoming election.

The English in the country are sometimes dismissed rudely by Afrikaners as *soutpiels* – salt dicks – with one foot in England and the other in South Africa. For unlike Afrikaners, they have an escape route if all the pessimists are proved right – passports that give them a refuge in England. Now they wait to see if they need to use them.

From *The Telegraph Magazine*
19th March 1994

(PS God had granted thirteen revelations of the northern half of the world and of South Africa concerning Unity to come and a united states of Africa? Perhaps one day?)

Friends, I was a little surprised to read this for it confirmed a vision granted here in Holy Cross Church some ten to fifteen years ago (recorded in our diary of Discovery and Revelations). For there I was standing in the balcony looking down upon the main body of the church, filled with people dressed in light attire and singing, looking up to the east and the altars. They were obviously from a hot country and a few women wore hats and, from the tanned colour of their skin, I thought them to be South Africans returning to their motherland? At that time I thought of my father's brother who died about the early 1930s in or close to Johannesburg.

We have now experienced almost twenty-one years of Divine Revelations concerning Unity of all branches of the One True Vine = Godhead III – by the year 2000.

4th April 1994

Yesterday we attended the Easter service at Framfield Parish Church. In the evening here I read from the Bible, Genesis v 16, 17, 18 before going to sleep. During the night God granted a vision to my soul of Clive's wife, Manjula's head, then the Godhead form with the All-seeing eye, then my son Clive's head on the right. For on Easter Monday eve they both returned from their honeymoon in Portugal. Thus God confirmed their marriage of brown and white – Unity.

15th April 1994

Twice during the night I heard three rat-a-tats as if on the front door. After the second one I looked out of our landing window but no human could be seen. The Devil again troubling me, I thought for it had appeared several times before at night, and also some knocks before.

Saturday 23rd April 1994

This evening there was a lovely rainbow high arched from my neighbour's farm stretching over the Framfield Road towards the Eastbourne Road.

24th April 1994

Last night after Bible reading I experienced a vision of a male human figure in a mask rather skeleton-like. Only three nights before there was granted a vision of a man in a tweed coat, a real human figure whom I know not nor can I recall.

At long last there is a change in the morning temperature and increasing sunshine. It was 63°F today and 62°F yesterday. The butterflies appeared in the garden. A Brimstone and a Red Admiral are gateways, I feel for them when they fly past. I have now commenced reading the New English Bible, the thirteenth Bible reading since the trance of July 18th 1976.

For three days now the citizens of South Africa have been voting for their government and a new president. Mr Nelson Mandela is expected to become the nation's first coloured president. I thus recall the Revelations of Africa granted to my soul.

1st May 1994

For three days we have had glorious sunshine here in the south with temperatures rising to 75°C and the flowers and hedgerows have now burst into bloom and the foliage of the trees have also burst open. Everywhere the bird Song has become enjoyable from early morning to late at night. For God's in the Heavens and His lovely world surrounds us now.

Yesterday we attended a service in the morning at the local Baptist Church and during the period when the Priest was preaching a rather comprehensive sermon, especially appealing to the children present when I noted a soft rainbow circle of light about three feet in diameter on the ceiling, above the preacher. At the end of the service I spoke of this to the minister who appeared surprised. A Revelation from God no doubt calling us all to return to the Bible = Unity. Perhaps also to have a greater concern for Bible teaching to children?

2nd May 1994

Today, the May Day holiday, birds were noticeably active over the three cross site. The collared doves frequently circled over and fly to and fro, west to east or east to west over the three cross site. This afternoon a pair of geese flew low overhead east to west and gabbled loudly just as I looked up. Many small Song birds were also gaily singing all the day through. The temp today was just 60°F.

Later in the day three collared doves flew west to east over the three cross site.

10th May 1994

All the people of the Government of South Africa voted today for a Democratic Party with Nelson Mandela as their president. A brown dragonfly settled on our south terrace close by me today, in the sunshine.

Later a pair of sparrow hawks circled overhead over the site of the three crosses, hovering.

Eight swallows from Africa, I believe, flew over the three cross site from the south, yesterday, and last week a few martins (three) flew over the three cross site here.

We are rapidly approaching the end of twenty-one years of Divine Revelations and the many calls from our Godhead III to all to return to the Bible, the prime source of healing, and grace and loving Unity = One Church in Unity to come.

I had expected the visions to cease on the twenty-first anniversary on 15 June 1994. Yet God alone is in control. This morning, Christ's mark on my left wrist was thirteen, by midday it had changed to the symbol 'R', Resurrection (born again citizens no doubt).

Our son Clive and his wife Manjula and family are now on holiday in Devon, the county of my birth. For we are in the third week of

May. It is glorious sunshine with frequent temperatures of eighty to eighty-four degrees each day, for the butterflies in our wild paddock of two acres have grown in great numbers now, for several months I believe.

Wednesday 11th May 1994

Although there was a partial eclipse of the sun yesterday the temp reached about 70°F today, and all the birds were Joyfully singing in the garden and hedgerows. All day long the collared doves were most active sitting on the treetops cooing softly, or flying to and fro over our house or the garden. The starlings were also busy flying west to east, or south to north. For the new South African government has now been established under the new president, Nelson Mandela.

17th June 1994

A large soft rainbow circle around the sun about 5 p.m. today.

21st June 1994

At night after Bible reading, God granted a very bright human-like vision of my niece Katrina living and farming in France. She appeared standing close by the Bibles at our bedside. I awoke suddenly and Beth was surprised as I suddenly sat up in bed after being asleep. A day later I sent her some photocopies and writings concerning the visions. We recall her husband, Luke, when he used to come to her father's farmhouse at Ripe.

For the Revelations commenced with a vision of a pair of hands writing on an A4 sheet of paper, I believe, in 1973. Also I was granted a vision of Jesus' head being painted by a brush held by an unrevealed hand – the Hand of God. So now I trust I may experience a period of rest after twenty-one years of great mental activity, and the Eternal Glory, of Divine Revelations. For I have almost completed our *Diary of Discovery and Revelation*.

24th July 1994

Last week Beth was granted a vision of a golden light over my head when I was asleep. Last week Beth was also granted a vision of her cousin Freda (her son is a doctor).

A few weeks ago God granted a vision of Ireland as a *whole*, soft grey light (Unity to come).

Come the 15th June 1994, I will have been blessed with over one hundred and seventy-five Divine revelations. Early this year after Bible reading, God granted this lovely poem embracing all the visions:

"There is a Light more bright than the midday sun or the moon and stars by night, for it is the light of Him who Loves us all as One. One Holy Church of Love." (A prayer of Unity, for all the revelations foretell Unity by the year 2000).

On Saturday 26th March 1994 Beth and I attended our son Clive's wedding to Manjula and at 3.30 p.m. that day we shared in the blessing at St Saviour's Church, Guildford, Surrey, on the original Pilgrims' Way, Canterbury to Winchester. God granted us a lovely day of sunshine throughout.

On Easter Day, Beth and I attended the Easter Service held in Framfield Parish Church, here on the South Pilgrim's Way. At night, after Bible reading, we prayed for Clive and Manjula on their honeymoon in Portugal. Later God granted to my soul a colour vision of Manjula's head on the left, then central, the All-Seeing Eye of God, the single head of the Godhead form which was granted, with Clive's head on the right. As Manjula's family originated in Sri Lanka, I felt that God has thus confirmed their marriage of Unity of Love, the North with the South.

On Wednesday, 30th March, we attended my brother Horace's funeral at Ringmer Parish Church at 10 a.m. For he died suddenly (aged seventy-nine) just before my own birthday on the 31st March this year. We shall all miss him for many a day, for he was my third brother to depart from our family.